Cheers to
Handling it!

Arun
2020

SHE HANDLED IT, SO CAN YOU!

AN INSPIRING AND EMPOWERING FINANCIAL GUIDE FOR WOMEN

ARWEN BECKER

LIFE
WITH *Arwen*
CHANGING THE WORLD ONE WOMAN AT A TIME

WHAT OTHERS ARE SAYING ABOUT
SHE HANDLED IT, SO CAN YOU!

"When I started reading She Handled It, So Can You!, I simply could not put it down. While women are known for putting everyone else first, Arwen ripped open the curtain to show you what's really happening. She gives you **the what, the why,** *and most importantly* **the how** *to position yourself as a woman armed with the education to be financially savvy and happy. It is the newest tool in my toolbox."*

— JUDY HOBERMAN, iHEART RADIO AND PODCAST HOST OF
SELLING IN A SKIRT, TEDX SPEAKER, AND BESTSELLING
AUTHOR OF *WALKING ON THE GLASS FLOOR*

"Arwen, you did it! When one has grown weary of stereotypical stories about women and money—then this book is the one you need. Most stories about women and their money are narrated like a scary dream: If you spend money, then watch out—you'll become a bag lady. If you save money, then guess what–you did not save enough money. In She Handled It, So Can You!, Arwen shares true stories that include growing your money confidence, the importance of investment persistence, the critical need of longevity planning today, and ultimately relishing your work. Do yourself a favor: Take a weekend, read the book, and start working on your money plan. Friends, you deserve this!"

— SHERYL BROWN-HICKERSON, CEO OF FEMALES & FINANCE,
NATIONAL SPEAKER, AND HOST OF *THE F WORD* PODCAST

"Women are so much stronger than they think! Having been in the male-dominated mortgage-lending industry for thirty-five-plus years, I take my knowledge for granted. What Arwen does in this book helps ALL women. Her practical stories and simple explanations will help any reader have the confidence to take action toward their financial dreams. Ladies, get this book into the hands of your daughters right now!"

— JEN DU PLESSIS, NATIONAL SPEAKER, PODCAST HOST,
MORTGAGE MASTERY MENTOR, CEO OF KINETIC SPARK CONSULTING

"Arwen's passion to lead women is like none other. She loves deeply; she encourages, inspires, and challenges us ladies all to live life to its fullest. She Handled It, So Can You! is a must-read; Arwen will move your heart. She will inspire your life and teach you solid financial principles to empower you!"

"Reading this book is like sitting down to share a bottle of wine with your best girlfriend. Arwen turns boring spreadsheets and cold numbers into funny, raw, and real stories that inspire and inform. By the time you're done, you'll have learned how to navigate the sometimes confusing, often intimidating, and mostly male-dominated world of finance like a pro. Every woman who has ever struggled to make sense of her finances needs to read this book!"

"The brilliance of this book lies not just in Arwen's storytelling, but in her ability to shine a light on the underlying dynamics that drive women to make crucial money mistakes. She lays herself on the page, allowing women the permission to take their own inventory without the often-associated guilt and shame, and at the same time holds their feet to the fire to do something different. Then, she tells them exactly what to do. If you want a gentle, instructional, yet highly entertaining kick in the ass, this book is for you!"

"Arwen is not only smart but also very caring. Her commitment to level up women not only in their finances but in their life is truly admirable. This book will give you the confidence to know that you are not alone and that no matter where you are you can win in your finances and in life. This book gives you permission to want something bigger for yourself and all other women around you."

"It takes an incredibly bright, intelligent, passionate, and courageous person to take a stand for positive change. In this refreshing book, Arwen takes a strong stand for all women—and it came at a critical time. You won't just learn impressive but practical financial strategies, you'll develop mature core values and thought leadership that will seal your transformation. Win the New Game with Arwen's guide."

— AMBER VILHAUER, INDUSTRY'S LEADING DIGITAL MARKETING SPECIALIST, OWNER OF NGNG ENTERPRISES, INC.

"Arwen shines a bright light into an arena that is usually kept dark for women. Reading her words is like talking to your best friend, big sister, and trusted mentor all at once. Arwen is a natural teacher and her soulful wisdom will leave you feeling inspired and ready to take control of your finances—once and for all!"

— KELSEY ERICKSON, CAREER AND LIFE COACH FOR DRIVEN MILLENNIAL PROFESSIONALS, FOUNDER OF EVERME COACHING

"I count the day I heard Arwen speak as one of the key turning points in my life. I went from being vaguely ashamed about my financial situation to having a pathway to a plan! No jargon—just heart-filled passion to guide me toward an approach for the rest of my life. Arwen's passion for delivering actionable and smart financial know-how to women burns bright white. It is unstoppable. Her logical is irrefutable, and even the kicks on the shin are delivered with compassionate accuracy! Read this book and get bounced out of your complacency!"

— ALAYNE REESBERG, SENIOR TECHNOLOGY COMMUNICATIONS MAVEN

"Arwen is a lady on a mission to empower women in a male-dominated industry. She has lived through, and genuinely understands, the financial pitfalls that women uniquely face. Arwen's perspective and authenticity are what make her new book so refreshing. She Handled It, So Can You! will inspire you to take the action that will change the course of your life indefinitely!"

— WENDY POSILLICO, MINDSET COACH, SPEAKER, AND FOUNDER OF STRANDS OF STRENGTH

"Arwen's approach to finance and life is inspiring and insightful. I love the journey she shares to help other women understand the power we hold in our own lives."

— KERSTIN O'SHIELDS, NATION'S LEADING BODY LANGUAGE STRATEGIST, NATIONAL SPEAKER, PERFORMING SOPRANO, AND FOUNDER OF THE BODY LANGUAGE STRATEGY ACADEMY

"I heard Arwen speak in my twenties. I had the pleasure to talk with her and she treated me with respect, listened, and gave empowering encouragement. As a missionary, I need to have a plan now for my future. I used to think if I didn't make a lot of money, I couldn't have a good retirement plan, but thanks to Arwen's wisdom in She Handled It, So Can You!—I know I can, too!"

– NATALIE STEPHENS HERRINGTON, AUTHOR OF THE FORGOTTEN ONES, STUDENT LIFE DIRECTOR AT COMPASSIONATE HOPE FOUNDATION

"I have known Arwen for over fifteen years; she has always had this way of communicating practical ways of taking charge of your financial, physical, and emotional health by simply exampling what it looks like, not just talking about it. This book takes powerful lived experience, tested and practiced habits and makes it relevant to the real-life woman of today. She takes the phrase 'living your best life' and shows you how attainable and achievable it really is. This book will be a game changer to whoever picks it up and decides they need and want something better!"

– FAHREN JOHNSON, YOUTH & COMMUNITY ADVOCATE, ARTIST, AUTHOR OF A VIEW OF REDEMPTION

"In She Handled It, So Can You!, Arwen strips away the mysteries about money, personal finance, and investing so that you feel empowered and inspired to take action today. Sharing best practices through her own relatable experiences guides you to understanding your next best financial step."

– DEBBIE PAGE, ENTREPRENEUR, BUSINESS COACH, AND LEADING AUTHORITY ON CASH FLOW AND PROFITABILITY FOR WOMEN BUSINESS OWNERS

DEDICATION

This book is dedicated to women who have "handled it" at some point along the way. To the women who have wondered, "Is it too late for me?" or "Will I be okay?" To those who have felt dismissed or talked over in the area of finance. To women who have ever felt a twinge of embarrassment that they don't understand "this money thing" or who wonder if they ever will.

Your anxiety and embarrassment stop today. Confidence will abound. I promise to leave you better than I found you.

And to my mom, Donna, thank you for showing me, through example, how powerful women are and how capable they are of rewriting their futures.

TABLE OF CONTENTS

INTRODUCTION

> *You're a fighter. You're stronger than you know. Just don't give up.*

SHE HANDLED IT

"Your mom doesn't have a credit card? How?" I felt so small when the popular seventh-grade girl—complete with designer clothes and expensive shoes—smirked after telling me we should go to the mall and shop. After foreclosure forced our family from my childhood home into a rental, I arrived on my first day of seventh grade and quickly realized the other girls' clothes weren't handmade like mine.

Neither my father nor my stepdad could provide for us financially. So, my mom did what most mothers do. She handled it. She handled it by working a job she despised as a lunch lady at the rival junior high. Her job provided us medical benefits, she had the same days off as my sister and me, and we had new *handmade* clothes.

Handmade is perfectly fine for biscuits, cards, and cookies, but for seventh graders, handmade is the worst kind of clothing. Lame. Broke. Lesser than.

Hold on for a second here; please don't misunderstand me. At forty-five, I am so grateful for what I did have, and for what my parents and community provided. All things considered, I had a very blessed life. I was fortunate to have a roof over my head, food on the table, people who loved me, and a safe place to attend school and play sports. Goodness knows other children didn't and don't have even those assurances. I did not have to deal with racial inequity or bias. But at that moment in time, I was an immature and self-consumed junior high kid, comparing my life to what I saw around me. As a twelve-year-old girl or even as a teenager, I didn't have the wisdom and appreciation of the three decades that would follow to truly understand the privileged life I had even as I struggled to fit in financially with my peers. For me, as a young girl growing up surrounded by families who had much more disposable income than mine, I felt constantly reminded of what I didn't have instead of seeing my many blessings.

My blessings included that my mom was—and is—an amazing seamstress. I remember walking through fabric stores and helping decide what "cool" fabric she would use to make my next outfit. I would beg her to purchase something more expensive, and often caused considerably more work for her with my pattern choices.

The memories are etched into my mind: glaring fluorescents shining on the fabrics and the old ladies who worked there (in fairness, everyone is old when you're twelve). Above all, I remember the walls of taupe file cabinets filled with patterns for that one perfect, beautiful dress my mother would make me for the upcoming dance. Sitting at the tables, I would flip through the books, admiring all the models, and pray that my mom could make "that one" dress I thought was perfect.

She could. She always could.

She was and is incredible at sewing. I had every color and pattern of spandex known to man during that time (ah, the 1980s). And alterations, geez, she worked magic! That was fantastic during the late eighties, when we wanted our jeans skintight, so much so that we needed someone else to help pull them off at the end of the day (if they ever got wet, those babies were never coming off)! She never had to say "no" for difficulty, only for the price to buy the pattern and the fabric to go along with it. Tragically, sewing is not hereditary. I can't even sew a hem.

Deep down, I relished the fact that she made stunning dresses with luscious fabrics—they always fit like a glove, and I knew I'd never run into a "who wore it best" situation. She made all four of my homecoming dresses, my junior prom dress, and my wedding dress! My wedding dress pattern was plain at best, so Mom dazzled it up by hand-sewing hundreds of crystals and fabric flowers, most of which went on the train that I wore for only thirty minutes or so during the ceremony. After thirty-some hours enhancing that dress, Mom said she would never do it again, no matter how much someone paid!

That is the love of a mother, the gift of a mom; my mom.

Thinking back to middle school, as much as I admired my mom, I was still embarrassed when other girls would compliment me, then ask me where I bought my outfit. I felt shame that we didn't have the money to buy it from the mall, even though it was made better and fit perfectly. I ached desperately to go to the mall and pick out an outfit like all my friends had, or buy a shirt at Guess that declared G-U-E-S-S in huge letters right across the front. That would prove that my mom didn't make it. To this day, I can't stand shopping at the mall because I have such terrible memories of going and not being able to afford anything more than $20.

Shame, anger, and resentment began to build. It was so unfair.

MONEY WAS ALWAYS AN ISSUE

More than once at Christmastime, my sister, Mindi, and I wrapped shoeboxes with pennies and nickels hidden inside, pretending we had lots of gifts under the tree. I clearly recall my mom and stepdad getting so frustrated, they stopped unwrapping those boxes and just tossed the "gifts" into our wood-burning fireplace. Mindi and

I watched in disappointment as the neatly wrapped, colorful boxes went up in flames, our change still inside.

But Christmas wasn't the only difficult time. The one thing I resented the most was when the phone would ring at dinner. This was before caller ID. I would jump up to answer, thinking it would be one of my friends. Instead, it was often a stern man with a demanding tone. "May I speak to your mother?" I would hold the phone out to her, and she would whisper while waving her hands: "I'm not here! Tell him I'm not here!" Invariably, the person on the phone was another bill collector.

No matter how hard my mom worked, we had a tough time. There weren't family vacations or a home of our own, but there were food stamps. And there was the rattling old blue Datsun that picked us up from school and took us to Value Village to purchase secondhand clothing. And there was the rental house that never felt like the kind of home I could comfortably invite friends to.

With no reliable father figure, no financial security, and no spiritual guidance, I sought to fill the void with sports and school, any way to receive an "atta girl" via MVP awards or stellar report cards.

The classroom and athletic field were two areas where I could control my situation and receive positive feedback that made me feel good, if only for a moment.

I was never the best in the traditional sense at school—I failed my first SAT exam (whoops)—but I worked hard and graduated with honors and a 3.9 GPA. Similarly, other girls were more naturally gifted athletes than myself, but relentless practice can get you far, and I was voted most athletic in a 4-A school of 1,500 students. I set records in swimming, went to state twice in softball and once in track, and was named volleyball MVP in the state of Washington my senior year. Girls who likely had more talent couldn't keep up with my drive—I drilled nights, weekends, and mornings for that recognition, to feel valuable and important.

Unfortunately, affirmations don't pay the bills. My hyper-planning brain worked overtime to find a way out of a life that was always monetarily lacking. Even babysitting twenty-three out of thirty days a month, each summer, wasn't enough to resolve my aching insecurity.

ALL SOLID PLANS START WITH BLUEPRINTS, OR IS THAT BLUE EYES?

By the time I got into high school, I had the perfect plan for my life. I was not going to have to struggle with money, *ever*. My brilliant fifteen-year-old idea was to find a nice, financially secure boy and marry him. Foolproof.

I was fifteen years old, a sophomore at Juanita High School in Kirkland, Washington, when my friends introduced me to a tall, young man with bright blue eyes. Success was written all over him; it was in his DNA. He was a born salesman, and when I looked at him, I saw my future financial security and peace of mind. We dated through high school, and as graduation neared, I received full-ride scholarship offers to play volleyball at the University of South Florida and Colorado State University. He signed on to play baseball with the University of Washington.

Dilemma.

With the full wisdom of my seventeen years, I declared, "I'm going to UW!" and listened as the air was sucked out of the room by the collective gasps of my mother and select volleyball coaches.

They gently and not-so-gently presented the drawbacks to my plan: I was forfeiting two full-ride scholarship offers, pinning major life decisions on a high school boyfriend, making short-sighted and immature choices.

I was determined to prove them wrong.

I graduated from college and was the first at everything. First to get married. First to buy a brand-new car. First to buy a house.

My new husband was as instantly successful as I had imagined he would be, and there was no more rattling old blue Datsun for me—we bought a brand-new royal blue Lexus G300 off the showroom floor. As a child, the only vacation my family ever took was a week on the coast of Oregon. Now I hopped on planes to Puerto Rico, Mexico, Maui, the Virgin Islands, New York, and on. We were the youngest members of a prestigious private country club, even though I didn't know how to golf.

My hyper-focused brain had relaxed just the tiniest bit. My plan was working: Rich husband, lovely house, fab car, and my job was the job of my dreams.

LIONS AND TIGERS AND BEARS, OH MY!

Ever since I was five years old, my sole desire had been to work with animals. The question was, as what? Veterinarian work involved a lot of schooling and a confined office. Dolphin training seemed inhumane. Marine mammalogy was too specialized. I desired to be part of a greater mission that allowed me to work with many types of animals. Then I found it: wildlife rehabilitation.

When I graduated from UW with a B.S. in Zoology, I became the Assistant Clinic Director of a non-profit called Sarvey Wildlife Care Center in Arlington, Washington. Mine was one of only two paid roles, overseeing 110 volunteers who were passionate like me about caring for sick, injured, and orphaned animals. I supervised more than 200 animals every day, performing tasks such as cleaning wounds; assisting veterinarians with surgery; and suturing, stapling, and tube-feeding birds, mammals, and reptiles from across the state. On top of that, I trained volunteers, dealt with media, ran marketing campaigns, organized fundraising, scheduled educational events, and updated the board of directors.

I cared for every wild animal you could find in the state of Washington. Elephant seals, pelicans, bats, flying squirrels, grebes, loons, herons, turtles, snakes, beavers, falcons, butterflies (yes, people would bring us "injured" butterflies), hummingbirds, jays, and black bears…the list goes on. I even assisted in a blood transfusion between two bald eagles, owned an "unrelease-able" Eastern Gray squirrel, and was attacked by a 110-pound cougar (that story is in Chapter Ten). Imagine bottle-feeding river otters, bobcats, deer, skunks, porcupines, harbor seals, and raccoons.

This was my first glimpse into living a *rich* life. Not a moneyed life, necessarily, but a life full of wonder, passion, and devotion. A mission to help the helpless.

Each day began at the crack of dawn, and I jumped out of bed to drive forty-two miles and give all I had for ten-plus hours a day. It was not about money; it was about my calling, giving to something I believed in and being part of an effort larger than myself. The operation included more than a hundred people every week who sacrificed their time to volunteer and serve. I was fulfilled, fascinated, and captivated…it was the coolest job ever!

LIFE WAS PERFECT, UNTIL...

I proudly ticked the boxes off my "fix my life" to-do list. Find a driven young man? Check. Get married? Check. Buy a home? Check. Start a dream job? Check. Travel the world? Check. Money in the bank? Check. Bills paid? Check.

Happily ever after?

As the new millennium approached, the clinic director, the raptor specialist, and I drafted our thoughts for the board of directors, outlining how we might continue this twenty-five-year-old non-profit into the future. The founder, who battled cancer, was in failing health, and we feared the center could struggle if we didn't have a plan for succession when she died. We spent each waking moment living and breathing animal rescue, and were sure the board would love our proposal, our dedication, and our forward thinking.

Little did I know, a single blinking light on my voicemail recorder would forever alter the trajectory of my twenty-four-year-old life.

"Arwen, this is Gary. I have been hired as an outside attorney to inform you that you have been fired from Sarvey Wildlife. Let me remind you this is private property, and if you step foot back on the property, we will call the police. Thank you for understanding and your cooperation in this matter. Goodbye."

Devastation. Despair. Confusion.

The day before, my co-workers and I had overseen more than a hundred volunteers and had been responsible for the 300 animals in our care. In one moment, our work was done. It was the only job I have ever been fired from. It was also the only one that mattered to me.

What the heck, God?

The founder had seen our proposal as a power play, an attempted coup. Knowing people I admired were assuming the worst of me, and not having the chance to explain, was one of the single most painful experiences in my life. Four years later, when the founder died and the center wobbled and suffered without a succession plan, it was painful to watch. I am proud to say, however, that it survived, and Sarvey continues the work I found so fulfilling to this day.

DOWNWARD SPIRAL

Without my dream job, I became a stay-at-home wife. I filled my time attempting new dinner recipes, going to the gym, and struggling to find something that made me feel worthwhile. Life became a lukewarm *Groundhog's Day* of wake, spend, rinse, repeat. All the money we had couldn't give me a purpose or happiness.

I continued my trend of firsts: first to get divorced.

(I expand more on this story in a book that is a collection of wit and wisdom about life and work by women in business, Why Didn't Anybody Tell Me This Sh*t Before?, *collected and edited by Marcella Allison and Laura Gale. My story is called, "A Man is Not a Plan." You can purchase the book on Amazon.)*

PAIN WITH A PURPOSE

Divorcing was a painful way to realize I had never paid my own bills. I had never made my own friends. I had spent so much of my early life building around the lifestyle associated with my ex that I had never given much thought to my own identity.

That void was now more expansive than before. What was wrong with me? Why couldn't I just be happy?

As I was drawing off the money I was "awarded" in the divorce, I had extensive alone time in my strange new apartment. The hours of silence drew out moments of intense, pain-filled soul searching.

A friend introduced me to Amway—a network-based marketing company that specializes in consumables such as makeup, vitamins, paper towels, etc. The company pushed all members of the network in personal development, "requiring" a commitment to individual growth to draw other distributors into the company to work with you.

I began to consume books such as *7 Habits of Highly Effective People*, *The 5 Love Languages*, *Confidence and Power in Dealing with People*, *Don't Sweat the Small Stuff*, *How to Win Friends and Influence People*, *Being Happy*.

I began to expand and grow. It was terrifying and exhilarating to find myself so far outside of my comfort zone, but I was intrigued. One tiny source of irritation, however, was that many people who focused on personal growth and change persistently mentioned "God," and it needed to stop. Like, yesterday.

It was one serious drawback to me about Amway: Its culture embraced and encouraged a higher power. Events opened with prayers, and the program regularly incorporated Sunday morning church services. It repulsed me. Yet, I was making new friends. These were people I respected. They had marriages I admired. They were fun, and we laughed a lot! They had a peace and joy for life I needed and wanted so deeply. I ached to feel loved, valued, and purposeful.

I wanted to feel the security they emitted, even amid their own financial struggles. They were happy even when things weren't going right. Even though their bank accounts were empty, their lives were full, and I didn't understand it, but I wanted that kind of peace.

One of my new friends challenged me to begin studying books about spirituality and invited me to church. I began to realize God loved me, adored me, and designed me with a purpose. An unconditional love for a hurting and broke twenty-four-year-old divorcée?

Light. Worth. Purpose. Joy.

God flooded into my life in April of 2000, washing into the biggest hole in my existence. I began to feel more complete than I ever had, but with this realization came a different kind of weight, one I didn't have to carry alone, but that was still significant: I had a lot of changing to do.

SPIRITUAL GROWTH, DWINDLING BANK ACCOUNT

Being involved with Amway in the early 2000s had helped me network and develop, but I wasn't making money. And, while I was embracing the readings about feelings, empowerment, and joyful living, I wasn't reading the books about saving, investing, and developing financial skills. Books on the recommended reading list included *Rich Dad Poor Dad, Richest Man in Babylon, Think and Grow Rich*, and a new one to the list, *Smart Women Finish Rich*. One irony is I now regularly discuss *Smart Women Finish Rich* with my clients and became great friends with the author, David Bach...Oh how I wish I had read these books twenty years ago. They were about 401(k)s, IRAs, mutual funds, and other financial jargon, a.k.a. "men's stuff." Someone else should take care of that, I thought.

Although you would have thought my divorce would have opened my eyes to the need for financial education, I was still twenty-four. There was a *lot* of life ahead of me.

PASSION SET ASIDE, TIME TO START MAKING MONEY

As I said, I had never paid my own bills; my financial stipend from Sarvey Wildlife of $400/month had barely ever covered the cost of gas to get to the center. I knew my first goal had to be a job that would pay actual money that could cover my actual bills. It was an empowering and terrifying thought.

A friend in mortgage services reached out to me with what she thought was a tenuous lead. I was getting ready to start with a local temp agency, but she had bumped into a man at a Bellevue coffee shop who was in financial services. He was just starting his own firm after years of experience with big-box firms, and they exchanged cards. He mentioned in passing, "By the way, I'm still looking for some good help. If you know of anyone looking for a job, let me know!"

She gave me his information, and after my one and only job interview, I was hired.

I landed my first "real money-paying job," a concept that makes me wince as I consider the many stay-at-home moms who are frequently denigrated because they don't receive a paycheck. Work that improves the lives you influence is valuable. Money doesn't equate to living a "rich" life.

My new boss, Randy, and I began a quick friendship. I never would have dreamed, with my zoology degree, that I would take a job in financial services. In many ways, I saw how it could be exactly what I thought finance was: uptight, stuffy, and super boring. But the adviser who hired me could make a conservative atmosphere fun and interesting. He was a futuristic big-picture thinker, and my focused planner brain was the opposite. It was a tremendous fit, though. He sketched broad ideas, and I would follow it up with bulleted action points to bring his ideas to fruition.

Weirdly, the work scratched an itch I had for math and puzzles, for turning a problem over and over until I found a solution. My boss became my mentor and eventual business partner.

In October 2004, my stepdad walked me down the aisle to join Randy as his wife, cementing our partnership. It was by far the best day of my life! Not only were we building our practice, but we built our family as we became the parents to three amazing boys—Morgan, Ashton, and Easton.

A single encounter at a downtown Bellevue Starbucks created beauty from my ashes. God has a habit of doing that.

Yet, this isn't, "and then they lived Happily Ever After." Remember, "A man is not a financial plan." Marrying a financial adviser, I would learn, is not a substitute for standing on one's own two feet. I was still in my late twenties and beginning a new verse of the same song. If you'd like to skip to something that reads closer to happily ever after, go to Chapter Three, because it gets worse before it gets better.

MANY GREAT MALE ADVISERS RELISH SERVING WOMEN

My industry is male-heavy. Only about a third of financial advisers are women, and senior roles skew roughly 85 percent male.[1] Many attentive male advisers across this nation enjoy working with women and give them the attention they deserve. Randy was one of them. My husband was a wonder to watch. I always felt such pride as he sat with clients; watching Randy care for the ladies and families he served made me want to be a part of this profession for the long-term. For him, it wasn't just business; it was very much personal.

He'd sit with women who were married, widowed, single, or divorced. For each of them, he'd bridge the gap in her knowledge to help her understand and find peace in her finances. His table was an emotional roller coaster: I'd see grief as he talked to a woman who lost her husband of forty-two years just months before they had planned to retire, then watch the delicate balance of loss and renewal as he walked a recent divorcee through her new financial picture, and

1   Coryanne Hicks. *US News: Money. November 18, 2019. "Female Advisors Start Their Own Firms to Prosper."* https://money.usnews.com/financial-advisors/articles/female-financial-advisors-start-their-own-firms-to-prosper

experience a sense of wholeness as he coached a married woman to get both members of a couple on the same page for retirement.

His attitude pushed me to get my life and health insurance license in 2003, and later my securities Series 65, and has attracted other like-minded advisers, male and female, to our office.

Through his example, I saw firsthand that a woman doesn't necessarily need another female to advise her financially; neither does she need a man. She needs an adviser who will listen, take time to educate her and understand her, be present, openly communicate with her, and who will act in her best interest.

REHABBING INJURED ANIMALS TO INSPIRING WOMEN — NOT THAT DIFFERENT

I went from rehabbing broken animals, or critters that were just slightly off course, to doing that same thing for women in my community. As I gained perspective from watching Randy work, I began to realize quite a few things about women-focused planning for myself. Women are natural planners and doers—taking charge of their finances also means taking charge of their personal security, dreams, and goals. Women typically are the ones who get the unexpected call to care for those they love…a call amazing women like you always take!

This book is not the book that's going to break down the financial tools and ins and outs of industry terminology for retirees. That will come in time. This book is more about preparing to prepare, so it's okay if the mention of finance still gives you worry, confusion, or discomfort. We'll get there. One of my best friends, Fahren, works with at-risk youth in the Tacoma school district, and she frequently reminds me: A student who doesn't have their basic needs met (food, safety, shelter, clothing) will not be able to perform optimally at school. Challenges to our basic needs make other obstacles that much more insurmountable.

The same is true of financial empowerment for those of us in or nearing retirement.

You need basic nourishment with "financial food" before you are ready to open your mind to the more complex concepts you will eventually need to learn in your journey. This book is not filled with extensive financial gobbledygook, and it's not for sophisticated investors. This is for those of us who sit on the edge of our meetings with investment advisers or insurance people, nodding our heads and not wanting to say anything for fear of being looked at as stupid. It's for entry-level students of retirement planning, even those of us who may be rather reluctant students.

I applaud you for reading through, for wanting to avoid the mistakes I have made, for moving through the fear of the unknown. You're going to handle this.

> *It's time to get to work building something you're proud of.*

CHAPTER 1

WHY WOMEN

Not average; Exceptional.

VOMIT-COVERED INFANT: WOMEN ARE WIRED DIFFERENTLY

Somewhere in the air above Colorado Springs, I heard a woman yell, "Somebody, please help me!" I looked across Randy's lap and the aisle of our thirty-seater plane to see the massive turbulence had been too much for a brand-new mom; she had just thrown up all over her eight-week-old daughter. Panic filled her eyes, along with a horrifying embarrassment. We were on lockdown for the plane's descent, and she was in no position to help her baby or herself.

To Randy's shock, I reached past him for the baby girl, pulling the wailing vomit-laden infant across the aisle, across Randy's lap, and into my own.

Before her mother (or Randy, for that matter) could recover, a flight attendant yelled at me to put the baby back on the other side, as if shifting fifteen pounds across the aisle would bring down the whole plane. Utterly ridiculous.

Without hesitation, a woman across the aisle, one seat in front of the sick mother, held out her arms, "Give her to me!" Back over Randy the reeking infant went, and her new custodian held her until the plane landed, allowing her mother a moment to tend to herself.

The plane touched down, the passengers grabbed their bags, the mother scooped her baby up and rapidly deplaned, likely a puddle of embarrassment. Though she didn't thank me or even acknowledge those who had helped, it didn't trouble me—my reaction had been maternal, instinctive.

Randy, however, had difficulty trying to comprehend why I took the baby in the first place. He is a wonderful father to our three sons, but the idea of jumping into this lady's business was unfathomable.

Not to a mom. What motivated me that day is one of the deepest parts of womankind. It's something women, young and old, exhibit—a deep desire to care for and protect those who are vulnerable. Women do this without hesitation, even to their own detriment.

Randy couldn't quite empathize, but the concept wasn't totally foreign. He did know what an incredible mom looked like.

FOR RANDY, IT WAS PERSONAL

Randy grew up in Renton, Washington, in a traditional nuclear family of four: his mom, Nancy, his dad, John, and his older sister, Kim.

When Randy was born, his dad worked as an accountant and mom as a secretary at West Coast Airlines. His mother could type a hundred words per minute on a manual typewriter. She played the cello and piano beautifully. Their life was consistent, stable, and happy.

Shortly after Randy was born, Mom's vision began to blur. She figured it was just changing eyesight, no big deal, so she made her way into the eye doctor for a routine check-up. The results went beyond new glasses. She was diagnosed with progressive Multiple Sclerosis (MS). She was just twenty-six.

Randy has no memories of his mom walking unaided. Earlier in his life, when she had full use of her arms and hands, she walked with a cane. When Randy acted up, his mother would grab her cane, and like a scene from the *Gong Show*, hook some part of him and pull him into her arms, subduing the mischievous little boy. He found it quite amusing to try and stay just out of Mom's reach, but she was like a ninja with that cane. Somehow, she always captured her lively little boy.

Laughter abounded. Their personalities and senses of humor aligned. They were two peas in a pod. Life was still very good.

One day Mom lost her footing on the area rug as she walked into the kitchen. The wail that eight-year-old Randy heard from the backyard was terrifying. He sprinted into the kitchen to find Mom in agony on the floor and Dad on the phone with 911. The ambulance hurried her off to Valley Medical in Renton. Randy and Kim stayed behind with Grandma until Mom returned home the next day in a cast and wheelchair.

Mom had broken her right femur in the fall.

After several weeks had passed and the excitement of the strange (and sort of fun) wheelchair had worn off, Mom headed back to Valley Medical to have her cast removed. Yay! Everyone was relieved that life would return to normal without the irritation and difficulty the wheelchair created in 1973—decades before Americans with Disabilities Act regulations.

Excited, Randy ran to the front door as their car pulled into the driveway. Dad parked, walked around to the trunk, and, to Randy's confusion, pulled out the wheelchair.

"What is going on?" Randy thought. "I thought that thing was gone."

His parents set things straight with the kids that day.

"Kim, Randy," Dad began, "I am really sorry to tell you that the doctors have told us Mom will likely continue to be in the wheelchair. Unless one day there is a cure for MS. I am so sorry."

Life as they knew it would never be the same. They all ached for life to go back to the way it had been.

SHE DIDN'T LET IT STOP HER — NANCY HAD GREAT DETERMINATION AND FAITH

Of course, as a family they held on to hope and faith that one day Nancy would be healed, but that day never came while she was on earth. As her vile disease advanced, Nancy lost all use of her arms. She dealt with severe pain and physical discomfort. She was completely immobilized and often quite helpless. But what Randy witnessed was a woman who would rise above her difficulties and disability. She didn't want others' pity.

She handled it.

Nancy used her exceptional communication skills to do whatever she could to mother her children, be a loving wife, and aid her community with the abilities she had. She was involved with the PTA and received the Golden Acorn Award, given to a deserving parent for service to their school community. She joined the MS Society so she could help counsel and support newly diagnosed patients. She diligently practiced her faith and demonstrated resolve amidst her incredible trials.

Due to his mom's disease, part of Randy's upbringing put him in the role of caregiver. He helped his mom with everyday activities, like eating and using the bathroom, having to provide support in ways that not very many young boys would have to. But looking back at his experience, that's part of what has shaped him into the man he is today. He's caring and empathetic. He has a servant's heart, especially for women. He has undaunted determination and is filled with faith and hope.

JUST TELL ME I AM GOING TO BE OKAY — WOMEN HEAR AND SEE THINGS DIFFERENTLY

"Just tell me, am I going to be okay?"

A simple question, but it's not easy to answer. Yet, the ramifications of that answer can bring peace and solace to a woman's soul. Men often want the details of an investment's projected rate of return, internal allocations, asset management strategy, etc. The ladies we see don't want to be in the dark about these things, but ache to know the answer to that overarching question, "Am I going to be okay?"

Addressing these fears through proper planning may be an emotional process, filled with self-examination about core values and what truly matters. It should be void of the feel you get working with a used car salesman. At Becker Retirement Group, that's how we see planning—we've put a lot into maintaining a culture that prepares clients from heads AND hearts.

In my introduction, I elaborated on how watching Randy gave me a compassionate perspective about how women could be treated in finance. Yet, the further I dove into the financial industry in general, here were my observations:

- Men and women typically had different financial needs
- The investment tools and methods for satisfying those needs were largely the same
- Most financial advisers I saw generally treated men and women as "the same but different" in all the wrong ways
- Advisers often expected a woman to behave and plan like a man, and then spoke down to her when she didn't
- Advisers often neglected women's emotional concerns and unique monetary needs
- Married women were often overlooked, as advisers typically only addressed male spouses

I watched as Randy and our team—men and women—spoke with compassion about emotional subjects and how they intersect with money. And then I glanced around and saw that many others in our industry—again, men and women—approached planning in much the same way as the stereotypical scratching, belching gorilla-like men on an evening sitcom, but with the bonus of being armed with spreadsheets.

Financial planning is very much about your core values. It's a message I'll repeat until there's no longer breath in my lungs. You deserve better than a spreadsheet with projections. Just painting it pink or throwing on some flowers doesn't make it women-friendly.

At Becker Retirement Group, our financial advisers and retirement planning professionals have learned to get comfortable with their emotions. Tears, hugs, and revelations abound, and I have come to love it when a woman drops an expletive or two during our visit because it tells me that she feels safe at our table and within our four walls.

Safety. Security. Freedom of choice. Freedom of expression. Freedom to be wonderfully you.

You deserve this all. If you feel "less than" wherever you currently are, then shake that off and move on to where you'll be shown your worth.

The massive needs I saw in the area of women's planning moved me to pivot Becker Retirement Group to specialize with women, partner with professionals who feel the same, and to advocate for training other advisers nationally through *LIFE with Arwen, Inc.* (www.lifewitharwen.com). *Leaders Inspiring Financial Empowerment*, the origin of the "*LIFE*" acronym, is my effort to help other planners specifically focus their efforts on women-focused events in their communities. I think of the meaning of the word LIFE, and it evokes thoughts of growth, health, forward progress, and renewal…ideas we all benefit from when planning for our future.

ELDERLY POOR ARE MOSTLY FEMALE – TIME TO BE SELFISH

As I look back on my journey (or often more accurately, "battle") with money, I marvel at my mom's willingness to sacrifice so much of her current comfort and future financial security to meet my sister's and my needs. The more women I meet, be they in their forties or nineties or in between, the more universal this principle of self-sacrifice seems. My mom is one of the millions of selfless women who will do anything necessary to give their partners, children, grandchildren, and parents what they need, often at their own expense.

But in a fascinating twist, it is just as vital to them to *not* be a burden on their extended family. Ever.

It is a very perplexing dichotomy.

Women will sow all their seed, give away the harvest, yet never want to be left begging for assistance. Sadly though, it's often because of this deep desire to help loved ones, often at all costs, that women will give up all their financial security. You want others to be happy. You want them to have peace and not struggle. You want the best for them. It's so overwhelmingly noble to care for those who can't care for themselves, but we must be extraordinarily mindful that if we do that our entire lives, financially, we may become some of the many women living in poverty, something we are already much more likely than our male counterparts to do.[2]

I don't want that for you. You deserve better. You deserve safety. You deserve to see your loved ones happy, but must that come at a detriment to your own security? No. You know that.

If you love those around you and value those relationships, don't let your love make you a martyr. You can wake up and break whatever cycles are keeping you from having control of your own life. Being selfless doesn't have to set you up to be broke at eighty-two.

---

2   Congressional Research Service. July 1, 2019. "Poverty Among Americans Aged 65 and Older." https://fas. org/sgp/crs/misc/R45791.pdf

You are too valuable. Do you know that? You are. Walk in that truth. This is not the end. This is just the start of the very best years of your life.

GO EASY ON YOURSELF — DON'T COMPARE TO OTHERS

Susan had been a client of ours for three years prior to her retirement. She had worked as a nurse for nearly forty years and was *ready* to retire. She was tired of the physical work, being on her feet all day, the politics enveloping health care, and the massive changes that occurred in her industry during her career. What she still enjoyed was the money, but the toll it took on her body, feet, and mind had become too much.

She was ready.

That Monday, she was giddy. It was her first official day of retirement and she was eligible to roll over the remaining portion of her company retirement plan, her 403(b). She was elated and grinning ear to ear from the moment that she ordered her chai tea latte from our client concierge. As she walked down the hall, she chatted about how wonderful it was to finally retire. Heaven!

During our conference call with her 403(b) provider, we bantered gleefully, teasing the customer service rep and laughing together, basking in Susan's joy of the moment. We scheduled a follow-up visit for the following Monday to finalize the last bits of her exit from "working life."

The week passed, and Susan was back in our office for the next visit. The look on Susan's face when I came out to see her sitting on the couch told a very different story. Something had changed. With a concerned look, I welcomed her into the privacy of one of our conference rooms. She sat right down at the table, and I made my way to the other side and said, "Susan, how are things going?" She burst into tears, reached over to grab a tissue from the center of the table, and blurted out, "I was not ready for this. This is harder than I thought. I miss my friends."

CHANGE IS BITTERSWEET

No matter how exciting the next season of life is for you, you almost always leave something great behind.

It's bittersweet.

Like raising kids. It is exciting to be done with diapers, but you miss those quiet snuggles of an infant lying against your chest. It is fantastic when that cute three-year-old toddler hangs on your every word, thinks you're a superhero, and screams with excitement when you walk through the front door. But then, the same kid innocently sneaks away to draw with a thick, green permanent marker on your light-colored carpet, in the center of the stairs, as well as on their pale face, blonde head, and one-year-old baby brother. Argh!

In retirement, you're happy to be done with the grind, or being told what to do and when, or the pressure created by your workload. But you often have friends and routines that get left behind, and this can leave you feeling idle and less valuable to the world around you.

Go easy on yourself. Don't compare yourself to anyone else. They may be further along in their journey or have different values or goals. Most importantly, you must spend some quality time contemplating the meaningful work you want to do in your next season of life. You must have a vision beyond retirement. As scripture says, "A woman without vision will perish." Build a vision board. Post pictures of the adventures or work you want to do now. Begin thinking about the value you will bring to others once you leave your formalized employment.

This is your time to write the next *chapter* any way you desire. Your canvas is blank, and you have every color in the palette; let the paint fly! Get dirty; it's way more exciting and colorful!

PLEASE DON'T GET ME WRONG — YOU MAY BE A FINANCIAL NINJA

Becker Retirement Group and *LIFE with Arwen* are here to help change the narrative of women and their relationships with money.. Women deserve to understand what's going on in their finances and deserve the utmost care and attention from their advisers.

The stories I tell and the situations I see are varied. I don't mean to imply with my message that women are inherently disengaged from their finances. I often sit with women who have a tremendous grasp of what's going in their financial lives. Maybe you are one of them and you understand your finances in full. Well done, girl! Perhaps you're married, and you're the Financial Alpha who balances the checkbook and can tell what percentage your brokerage account earned last year. If that's who you are, partnering with an engaged retirement planner can take you from *good* to *great* in this unique season.

One woman asked after an event, "I have owned a mortgage company, overseen my own investments all my life, and I've done really well. What could you even do for me?"

"You have done what many women I meet with haven't; you have your finances all in line, so congratulations! Great job!" I responded. "But one thing you have never done is retired anyone, including yourself. My company and I have done it for twenty years, successfully, and my husband for thirty-two years. The part I am most proud of is retiring ladies through the years of the Great Recession and keeping them retired and peacefully doing life the way they want."

You may be incredible at saving and accumulating assets. Still, I have seen some big mistakes made early in retirement that have devastating consequences when ladies apply the same "game plan" that got them to retirement. That plan might not get you through retirement. Let me repeat that in a different way. The game and the rules change the moment you stop working. Make sure you hire a coach to help you get it right from the very start, before you pull a hamstring or worse, blow out a knee and perhaps even end your career (a.k.a. your financial peace in retirement).

So, whether you know every detail about your finances or are starting in a place of perceived ignorance and embarrassment, we are going to tackle this journey together. I have only one job to do, *to leave you better than how I found you.* No one in your life deserves this more than you.

Let's do this!

> *Wisdom isn't something money can buy. It costs us time, effort, and focus.*

MOST IMPORTANT TAKEAWAYS

1. Women see and hear things differently. That's okay. You need an adviser who hears you and speaks to you in a way you understand.

2. 80 percent of the elderly poor are female. That will not be you with proper planning now.

3. No one else can do the preparation for you (a.k.a. a man is not a plan).

NEXT STEPS

1. Say this out loud, "Starting right now, (list today's date) _____/_____/20_____, I will walk in my inherent value and worth! I can handle this!"

2. Continue to read this book to be empowered and inspired to tackle this part of your life!

CHAPTER 2

VALUES-BASED PLANNING

Today is all you've been promised;
don't waste it.

IS BOEING WORTH A LIFE?

B oeing wants to be out of the pension business. They have begun offering many long-term employees a lump-sum pension buyout, in the hopes of ending their days as a long-term pension provider. Dick was one of those fortunate people. He enlisted our help to determine whether to leave the retirement funds at Boeing for them to distribute to him as a lifetime pension, or to take it as a lump sum.

Dick was seventy-one and had given forty-two years to this beloved, incredible, world-changing company.

He came in for our initial visit with his wife, Alice, who was seven years older and vibrant. She had bright curly hair and was a colorful dresser with a bubbly attitude. She was giddy and excited to start truly enjoying her retirement—she had been waiting for ten years after her own retirement for Dick to be "ready."

Their funds were healthy. Dick was not. As I watched Dick leave my office that first day following our initial visit, I knew something was not right. He struggled to get out of the chair and put his coat back on. When I watched him shuffle out of my office, my heart sank. All I could hear in my head was the question, *"Was Boeing worth it?"*

The weeks rolled into months as Dick and Alice transitioned into retirement. They moved into a new retirement community, made fast friends, and went on their first trip as a dually retired couple. A cruise to the Caribbean! At their next visit to our office, Alice marveled at how much fun it was and couldn't wait for their next trip to Europe. They were getting accustomed to retired life together.

Sadly, that next trip would never come.

Dick had been retired less than two years when he slipped while walking the dog, fell, and seriously injured his head. With blood pouring into his eyes, he stumbled back to his room, where Alice called for an ambulance.

As Dick was going in and out of consciousness, the staff at the intensive-care unit did what they could to stabilize him. Twenty-four hours after being admitted, in a near-miraculous moment of complete lucidity, Dick called for his wife, and they enjoyed a thirty-minute loving conversation. Dick told Alice once more of his deep devotion to her, that he had the most wonderful life with her, and that he loved her dearly. She was his everything.

It was a tremendous, precious gift from God. Dick died an hour later.

When Alice called us to let us know that he died, my heart sank for the second time. I didn't want to be right, but when you work for decades with retirees, you see patterns. Dick had given forty-two of his most productive and healthy years to a company. He generated nearly two million dollars in retirement savings. And for what? Less than two years of retirement?

But it happens all the time. Fear there won't be enough money causes people to work much longer than is needed or to give the best of themselves to their company, rather than to family or to pent-up dreams.

Dick had waited too long to truly live, leaving his lovely bride to handle it after he died.

One popular quote rings true: "People spend their health trying to gain wealth and then often spend their wealth trying to regain health." All the money in the world can't buy back the health those years have stolen. You have one trip around this planet and one body to do it in. Don't give the best of *you* to a company. Your family deserves that gift before retirement and after. I want to help you figure that out and get to the right mental space, so you get to enjoy life before *and* after retirement.

THE BEST YEARS OF YOUR LIFE — THE GO-GO YEARS

Please don't shoot the messenger. Okay? I'm not currently in this age range that I'm citing, but multiple studies have been done that state the best years of your life are between the ages of sixty and seventy-five. Hands down.[3]

You're smart. You kind of know why: You've got money. You've got time. If you're married, your spouse is likely still living. Your friends are still living. Grandkids are young enough, and they still want to spend time with you. You've got your health. You're able to go out and do things that you have been patiently waiting and dreaming of doing.

---

3   David G. Blanchflower. National Bureau of Economic Research. NBER Working Paper No. 26641, January 2020. "Is Happiness U-shaped Everywhere? Age and Subjective Well-being in 132 Countries." https://www.nber.org/papers/w26641

These are called the Go-Go Years.

Many of you reading this are older than seventy-five and still very much in the Go-Go mindset. That is wonderful. I work with many eighty-year-olds who are still vibrant, busy, and traveling. And then many of you may be in your forties like me and not be in that age range yet, but you have deliberately made the time and taken the chance to enjoy your time right now. I commend you. That is what we all ought to be doing, living our best life *now*.

Tomorrow isn't guaranteed for any of us, and every day that passes, health may dictate what we can and can't do. But I am trying to stir up those of you who are, like Dick, too afraid that you "won't have enough for the future" if you take some time right now to enjoy the life and the finances you have built toward your entire life. Please don't wait; get educated, meet with a retirement planner/adviser and, with help, you can find a way to enjoy your life right now *and* in the future.

PERMISSION TO SPEND YOUR MONEY

Spend now! Seriously? That's a tall order since you have worked at accumulating and saving for the last forty years. This may be the toughest hurdle you'll face nearing or just entering retirement. You have to trust your adviser's assessment and believe what the mathematical planning process says. If solid, holistic planning shows your life-long financial efforts have given you enough money to retire comfortably and cover the "what-ifs" (unknown span of life, future health care needs, a repeat of the Great Recession…etc.), it's high time to start living those pent-up dreams!

"How can you be sure I will be okay?" If this isn't the key question we must answer every day, then I don't know what is. Most women I sit with want to know they are going to be okay, meaning they want financial security through their whole lives (freedom, options), and want to know they won't ever be a burden on their kids (those wonderful people they sacrificed many of their years to care for). That's it. The deep concern in their hearts is, "Tell me I am going to be okay."

RETURN ON INVESTMENT (ROI) – MATH DOESN'T LIE

You've likely heard the term return on investment (ROI). An adviser sits with you bragging about how their investments posted a 10 percent average ROI over the past couple of years. Ooh, sounds good, right? Maybe you're thinking, "Math doesn't lie," and you'd be right. But just like your teacher always checked your work, when someone starts talking about averages, you should always look deeper.

For instance, if a couple jogs an average of twenty-five miles a week, you'd envision both people in tracksuits, up at the crack of dawn. But what if that average instead means one of them gets up when it's still dark and jogs ten miles every weekday morning for a total of fifty miles, and the other one stays in their pajamas and plays cat-and-mouse with the snooze button?

Let's see how the game of averages breaks down with ROI.

	SCENARIO ONE – MORE RISK/VOLATILITY		SCENARIO TWO – LESS RISK/VOLATILITY	
Year 0		$1,000,000		$1,000,000
Year 1 ROI	60% ROI	Add: $600,000	30% ROI	Add: $300,000
Total after Year 1:		$1,600,000		$1,300,000
Year 2 ROI	-40% ROI	Minus: $640,000	-10% ROI	Minus: $130,000
Total after Year 2:		$960,000		$1,170,000
Total ROI after 2 years:		10%		10%
10% ROI	60% - 40% = 20% divide by 2 years		30% - 10% = 20% divide by 2 years	

Do you see that, although both have a 10 percent average ROI, the final sums are quite different? Okay, now let's do it with more realistic numbers that a retiree might be hoping for:

	SCENARIO ONE – EMOTIONAL ROLLER COASTER		SCENARIO TWO –RELAXED	
Year 0		$1,000,000		$1,000,000
Year 1 ROI	15% ROI	Add: $150,000	8% ROI	Add: $80,000
Total after Year 1:		$1,150,000		$1,080,000
Year 2 ROI	-7% ROI	Minus: $80,500	0% ROI	Minus: $0
Total after Year 2:		$1,069,500		$1,080,000
Total ROI after 2 years:		4%		4%
4% ROI	15% - 7% = 8% divide by 2 years		8% - 0% = 8% divide by 2 years	

*Examples shown for illustrative purposes only
and don't reflect taxes or investment fees.*

Again, we have two portfolios with the same average ROI. Math doesn't lie. If you have the same ROI, but less volatility (the range in which the positive and negative numbers swing), you will *always* have more money in the end. It's pure mathematics, and reduces your degree of worry. If you're constantly striving for 10 percent, 12 percent, or more, but it's causing unnecessary volatility and an unending emotional roller coaster, it isn't worth it. Period.

When we are creating our *Best Life Retirement Plan*, we don't assume higher than a 7 percent ROI, even with our most aggressive professionally managed growth portfolios. We feel that would be irresponsible when running long-range scenarios. We want to show that your retirement could function well if your assets earn 3 to 7 percent with the added pressure of high inflation rates (3 percent or more) and low cost-of-living adjustments (COLAs) on your Social Security. We do this to pressure test your retirement plan from every direction. Make that baby strain and struggle. That way, we can have a sense of confidence that if you continue to manage your expenses as you are, the plan has been designed to work beautifully!

Math and responsibility collide.

What if you could have that same standard of living and lifestyle with less volatility, and enjoy a less stressful retirement? Wouldn't that feel a lot better? That is Return on *Retirement* (ROR).

RETURN ON RETIREMENT (ROR)

Let's look at the difference between ROI and ROR. Many advisers will talk about moving the money you have around in stocks, bonds, mutual funds, ETFs, REITs, variable annuities, indexed annuities, life insurance, etc. These are all tools; they aren't necessarily a plan. A great adviser will help you plan for, with an acceptable degree of certainty, a retirement in which all the money you've saved during your working years provides for *your* entire life (especially for you married women). They will help you design a strategy to cover your income needs, future health care, or death of a spouse, and then the dreams you've been waiting to fulfill once you retire. That last piece seems to be one that some advisers frequently overlook in the planning process.

You aren't here to "time the market" or chase returns. You're building a comprehensive plan based on conservative rates of expected return that helps you keep the money piece in the background, and your *best years* in the foreground. That's what we're striving for, and that is what you deserve after your years of hard work and sacrifice. The most important part of your planning is making sure those dreams you have for your life have a dollar figure attached to them and are illustrated and woven into your plan.

There is a big difference between *investing* versus *planning*, and the same applies to ROI versus ROR.

FOUNDATIONAL PILLARS OF A RETIREMENT PLAN

You may be afraid of losing in the market. Or concerned that you won't have enough income. Or you're bothered by the idea of losing purchasing power to inflation. I get it—those are the central points that we help people address every day.

Becker Retirement Group was built in September 1999 on three foundational pillars that follow a particular order. Our stepped approach aims to reduce the anxiety around each of these topics by explicitly addressing them head on.

The first pillar is ***preservation of assets***. You've worked your entire life to accumulate the money you have for retirement. We need to make sure that at least a portion of that money is protected and will be there throughout your entire life (not just for 90 percent of your life).

The second pillar is ***income planning***. Many of you will have some form of an income gap once you separate from work and are no longer collecting wages. The gap might be even more significant if you retire in your early sixties, Social Security hasn't kicked in, and you're paying hefty premiums for health insurance and related costs. We need to find a way to create guaranteed income, like when you were working, while helping you enjoy the fun stuff time affords you.

The third pillar is ***growth***. Growth is still a vital component of your retirement plan, especially as a woman, because that is what helps guard against longevity, inflation, and the cost of future health care. Growth can also help you leave a legacy to those you love. What we don't want is for growth to threaten the first two pillars, preservation of your assets and income. By putting growth in its proper place, we can invest for the future without having to think of the way tomorrow's market movement might affect your bill-paying abilities.

FULLY EMPOWERED TO IDENTIFY YOUR VALUES

If you first identify your core values, what matters deep in your soul, making financial decisions becomes a whole lot easier.

Just like planning in a micro-climate (more on this idea in Chapter Six), I see women decide how to spend their money without considering their bigger picture, or their values. It is vitally important to discover the deep need or value that you have inside your heart and soul, then align your finances to match that, rather than creating a "value" to justify your spending habits. That always leaves you feeling empty and unsatisfied.

This exercise is so important to the whole planning process because we want to make sure that anything that we use, any investments or products, have purpose and focus. It's critical that your financial plan is built on your core, intrinsic values—the big picture of life, not the next cool investment.

We are speaking to the *intangibles* (values): freedom, comfort, not being a burden on your family, choices, security, etc. Not the *tangibles* (goals): travel, boat, new car, golf, home in Arizona, etc. Those goals are all wonderful and exciting, but if they threaten your deep need to have financial security long-term, you won't ever have peace inside. You will be left with a searching soul, trying to find contentment that you won't find in tangible things (and you will likely begin to resent those items or the person who "coaxed" you into buying them).

This exercise is important for all, and particularly vital for couples. A lot of divorces stem from money disputes. Getting on the same page, value-wise—even if it means upsetting the applecart a bit to dig into your household finances—can make a difference in the longevity of both your savings and your relationship. A little discomfort today can mean comfort for decades into the future.

For those of you ladies who are married to women, getting on the same page also applies to you, and is vitally important to the health of your relationship. However, in our practices, we've seen discrepancies arise more between men and women and their differing mindsets and emotional approaches. Certainly, some men are more in touch with their emotions, and some women struggle to access theirs, but for now I'm going to elaborate on what we'd see as a "typical" contrast of men's and women's planning.

Seeing and understanding the *intangibles* is often a lot easier for women since they are typically more connected to their emotions and feelings, whereas men may have to work a bit harder to get to that same root. But don't be fooled; it exists inside of them. Men may need a bit more time to think and meditate on what money means to them since most of them have grown up being goal-focused. Be patient. If you are married to a woman, you may also find this to be an easier process for one of you, more so than the other.

When I host public events, I ask the audience, "What does money mean to you?" It is uncanny that about 99 percent of the time, women throw out words in the values/intangibles category, and men throw out goals and tangibles.

Men are just wired differently.

OOPS, I DID IT AGAIN

When I went to work for Randy after my divorce, I had a monthly check from my ex in payment for my half of our community property, and I had my paycheck from my job, and a tiny bit from my side hustle with Amway. I thought I was rollin' in the dough! Yet I still wasn't educating myself about finance as it might apply to me.

Randy had a large office, a warm and comfortable home, and all the trappings of success. His role was making the money for the business, and I aggressively supported that, running the administrative aspects of the business with an iron fist. I even stopped collecting a paycheck when we got engaged in 2004, figuring it was an unnecessary step in what would become our joint income. I was learning, in a very general way, about how to set people up for long-term financial success. I had it made (again)!

What I failed to see was that, only four years after my divorce, I had begun to slide back into "white knight" syndrome. Sure, I was dipping my feet into the pool of finance—though at that point I was not an adviser in any capacity—but I hadn't taken ownership of my money or my circumstances.

MECHANIC WHOSE CAR IS IN DISREPAIR

As I mentioned before, I was reading all the touchy-feely books on confidence, excellence, love, and faithfulness, but I never cracked even one book on money. I knew the basics of personal financial planning from a theoretical standpoint, of course, but that was still largely the realm of Randy. With fifteen years of experience, Randy was an impressive retirement professional. Why would I need to bother myself with our financial details?

Randy's upbringing was different from my own. His dad was an accountant who scraped to take care of Randy's mother through her battle with MS. My mom was a lunch lady who did her best to be mother, father, chauffeur, cook, and clean-up crew for my sister and me. We lived in the negative space left by both my father's and stepdad's various failings and mistakes. Teaching us about saving, investing, entrepreneurship, and the like was not even on the list.

I was a math whiz and took statistics in college just to stay sharp. But I didn't know anything about running a business, principal and interest, cash flow, taxation, or any of the rest of it. I figured that wasn't a big deal, that was Randy's job. Some of it was arrogance (It's not that hard, right? I'm smart. If I have to know it, I'll figure it out.) and some of it was regular neglect (Randy was crazy busy with clients, employees, and events—I figured I'd bother him about it later).

I have since learned, it's a tragically common situation in our line of work. But "keeping the peace" is little comfort when consequence comes knocking.

GREAT RECESSION

The worst stock market decline in my life, second-worst to the Great Depression, struck in September 2008. I know you can recall how that affected you and those around you. People lost jobs, homes, possessions, and the feeling of personal worth that goes with them. Granted, as I sit here doing my final edit, my entire community of Kirkland, Washington, is under a mandatory "shelter in place" order where nearly every business has closed due to COVID-19. I pray that the coronavirus pandemic doesn't turn into something worse than 2008, but if it does, we are confident that we have prepared our company's and our clients' plans as best we can. But the economic talk surrounding the market right now certainly gives me some flashbacks to the sort of discussions and financial decisions that were made in the Great Recession.

Owning a firm that manages wealth isn't pleasant in a recession. Overall, people have less wealth to manage. Even those who have plenty become reluctant to adjust their current plans. During the Great Recession, even our clients of twenty-plus years exhibited "analysis paralysis" in making any new changes within their retirement plans. Many of Randy's office hours were filled talking current clients through their fears, performing more of an emotional service than a financial one, and leaving no time to fill the appointment book with new clients. Over two years, that ricochet effect dwindled our income by 66 percent. Something had to give.

We decided that "something" was our personal residence, and, after eighteen months and three failed tries to renegotiate our home loan, we entered foreclosure proceedings.

Failure.

NUDE AND HUMILIATED

If you put this book down and walk away, or you decide you have nothing to learn from a financial adviser who was foreclosed on and was heavily in debt just ten years ago, I couldn't blame you.

To be sure, I had some serious low points. I laughed somewhat hysterically through tears at a bank employee, saying, "You can't take my kids, even if you take my car?" I sheepishly borrowed money from my twelve-year-old to gas up the car right before Christmas. I'll be the first to put up a hand if someone asks, "Who has ever been stupid about money?"

Yet. "Let him who is without sin among you be the first to throw a stone at her." When multiple men dragged a nude, humiliated woman out into the *public* square, having caught her in adultery, they wanted Jesus to condemn her to death by stoning her, which was the law during that time. I'm going to set the justice system of the thirties A.D. aside, as well as the ludicrous double-standard that allowed the adulterous man to remain anonymous, and instead face the fact that this woman in her adultery made a terrible choice, no question. But redemption is always possible if someone is willing to change. Jesus' response was not to excuse her adultery but to make everyone standing in judgment of her instead stand in judgment of themselves. Under the weight of their own scrutiny, they all failed. Everyone dropped their rocks, starting with the oldest (wisest).

We all fail. But we are called to change. This experience of what I saw as complete failure was my call to do what many women the world over have done since the dawn of humanity: I handled it.

Randy and I both recognized the need for change, and so we began the hard and harrowing work of change, side by side. No more blaming and fault-finding.

CHANGE IS A HUMBLING CHOICE YOU GET TO MAKE AT ANY TIME

Personal finance books, late-night conversations, spreadsheets, check-lists, meditations, purging belongings and unnecessary expenses, classes, business, and financial coaches: We quickly made changes. In six years, we went from a highly leveraged business carrying hundreds of thousands in tax obligations and debt to owning a home and two rental properties. With the exception of our mortgages, we were debt-free in our personal and professional lives. We owned our cars and had fully funded our retirements, insurance policies, and college 529 plans (a moment of self-congratulation as I mention that we just got one son through college completely debt-free). We had IRAs, Roth accounts, and other brokerage investments.

We implemented our new ways of thinking in the small things, and they compounded into huge, sweeping changes.

I have been dismissed, as a financial adviser, by prospective clients who found the public records about our foreclosure. I am not ashamed. We learned. We forfeited our personal home to make sure we maintained our business, which included the most important commitments to our clients and staff. I am proud, looking back, that we chose to continue as a company to serve and employ in our community, even if we suffered severe personal setbacks.

We humbled ourselves and got educated in areas where we were falling short. It's the same thing you are doing in choosing to read this book. You go, girl!

MONEY THERAPIST

As we read books and followed along in the workbooks many of them had, we discovered two eye-opening things:

1. We had an eighteen-point to-do list of things that we needed to tackle/update in our own financial lives and

2. We each saw *our* money from very different points of view.

My view and Randy's view of how to handle our finances were deeply rooted in our childhoods and histories.. At times, it felt like these financial book authors were acting as our "money therapists," something we often do for our own Becker Retirement Group clients, helping to get to the root of what matters and then focusing the plan around that. We had to *clearly* identify what we each valued about our money and then combine the two sets of values to anchor ourselves when making small and big financial decisions.

Sorry if I come across as a broken record, but, especially as a couple, this is more important than any of the planning you will do individually. Determine your values now.

I'm serious. Now.

Do. Not. Delay.

I sit down with too many women contemplating divorce over a fundamental difference in their and their spouses' approaches to money; it's awful. If Randy and I had continued on that path, that might have been our future, too. That is not going to be you. Don't passively sit back and wait. Get focused, deliberate, and diligent on this "money piece." You and your partner need to clearly identify what your values are by doing this exercise separately, then combining your responses into one list of values that makes both of you feel heard and puts you in agreement.

If a couple is not in agreement, at the very least, life will have turmoil and uncertainty. But in the worst case, the marriage will end because of money disagreements. No one wants that. Not your kids, your grandkids, or your friends, so it is worth a bit of "being uncomfortable" and tackling this often-difficult subject of money and values. A handful of arguments are much easier to deal with than a divorce, and they're a lot less costly emotionally, mentally, and financially.

I urge you to get this done in the next couple of weeks because it makes this whole planning process a lot easier.

I believe in you, and your relationship is worth it!

GETTING TO THE CORE OF THE MATTER

Stop here! Grab a pencil or pen.

I really don't want you to go any further in this book without taking a few minutes to do this exercise. Grab a pencil and start filling in the blanks right in this book (or if you are reading this on an e-reader, grab a journal or piece of paper).

This exercise is the start to changing your life. Some women will skip past this, but you won't. You want to change. You want something better for yourself and your life. You can handle this.

Now ask yourself, "What does money mean to me? What are the feelings I sense when I think about having money in my accounts?" (Checkmark, highlight, star, circle, whatever you prefer, denote those that matter to you.)

Note: This same exercise is available at the back of the book for your partner. You can then compare your responses.

+ Security
+ Control
+ Freedom
+ Fun
+ Safety
+ Options
+ Personal Strength
+ Power
+ Influence
+ Peace
+ Good health
+ Not being a burden on my kids
+ Time with my family
+ Time with my friends
+ Ability to volunteer
+ _____ (write here)

Think some more. Probe deeper for anything not on the list.

+ _____ (write here)
+ _____ (write here)
+ _____ (write here)

(If you are part of a couple, STOP HERE. Do not complete the top five below until your partner has done their own list.)

Now I want you to list your top five core values below. If you do this as a couple, show each other what you wrote and discuss the best way to blend those values into a list of five.

My/Our top five core values are:

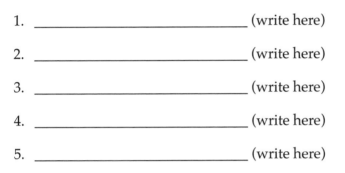

1. _____ (write here)

2. _____ (write here)

3. _____ (write here)

4. _____ (write here)

5. _____ (write here)

These five should really speak to the core of what matters to you. When you say them out loud, these words should evoke feelings deep inside that empower you to feel content and secure. When you close your eyes and imagine those words, a sense of peace and inspiration should wash over you. *That* is what we need to help you make financial decisions based on material in the remainder of this book.

By relying on core truths and values, you can ask yourself, "Does this financial decision get me closer to those five core values, or move me further away?" If it is the latter, you want to make a different choice.

Now that you have the most important piece identified, it's time to rock this thing called life!

> *At any moment, you can choose a fresh start.*

MOST IMPORTANT TAKEAWAYS

1. Return on Retirement (ROR) is what you are seeking. It's about peace of mind more than Return on Investment (ROI).

2. We all fall short at times, but "getting back up" is always your choice.

3. When you identify your core values, making financial decisions becomes a lot simpler.

   Couples need to identify core values to gain an understanding of what matters most to both partners and how your core values compare.

NEXT STEPS

1. Run through the values exercise before going on to the next chapter. If you need to wait for a partner/spouse, determine what date you will have it done by: ___/___/_____.

2. Take these top five values and write them, right now, in ink on the inside front cover of this book (or put a little card in your wallet), so you can easily access what really matters to you when faced with financial decisions.

CHAPTER 3

GOOD NEWS

*Stop comparing your blooper reel
with others' highlight reel.*

NO MORE HAIR NETS

"Oh my God, what if it doesn't work?" These words swirled around the mind of a careful, calculating, and hard-working mom of two. Once my mom hit forty-three years old (my age today as I type), and both my sister and I had graduated from high school, she'd had enough of living paycheck to paycheck.

My father was tens of thousands behind in child support, and even more so in meaningful visits, yet she didn't spend her days trying to collect or hiring costly attorneys (or bad-mouthing him to us). She just got up and went to work. Every day. She was at work by 5 a.m., preparing food for a bunch of ungrateful junior high kids, slaving away in a hot kitchen, overcoming her aching feet and back, all to receive a measly paycheck and be home by 2:30 p.m. so her daughters had a mom around for homework, chores, athletics, and attention.

My stepdad did little to assist in making her life easier. She took care of dinner, chores, discipline, shuttling me to hundreds of hours of practices and games, and keeping the house as tidy as she could. Financially, she bore nearly all the responsibility, and quite often her husband added to the struggle by trying to avoid the IRS. Once the government garnished her wages to pay for his poor choices.

Is there any chance for redemption? Hell yes! She is a woman. She is a mother. She is a warrior. She saved and sacrificed. She handled it.

She declared, "enough is enough." With both of us girls out of the house, she took a leap of faith and left the lunchroom for a seasonal job at Costco. There were no guarantees. It was a pay cut with a longer commute and no benefits. But she rolled the dice.

Since her only skills were in food service, she went to work during the 1998 holiday season in the little food court at the Costco adjacent to their corporate office in Issaquah, Washington. She was exhausted from doing that kind of work, and she hated it. Her feet hurt and the work was grueling, but those were the skills she had. That was it. She was tenacious and confident enough to believe her work ethic would shine so brightly that they couldn't think to let her go once the Christmas season was over.

Jackpot! Well, sort of.

Costco couldn't live without her, this was true. She was a gem. The kind of employee you pray to add to your team. The player who makes everyone around them work a bit harder, longer, and with greater integrity. The company formalized her employment to full-time in the food court and eventually promoted her to manager. "Oh yay, more years in foodservice." Ugh.

It was never her intention to continue making pizzas or grilling Polish dogs, refilling ketchup containers, cleaning up the large metal tables after they'd been trashed by toddlers, or worse yet, teens who didn't care how messy the table was after they snarfed down their cheap eats. But she stayed faithful to the course she believed in.

After one full year doing this undesired work, Mom put in an application for a higher position, pulled the Vegas slots lever, and rolled the magical triple 7s.

"Donna, we're offering you a position in the corporate office." *No more hair nets*!

With the thousands and thousands of employees Costco has, I doubt it could find many other employees who are as honest, hardworking, and consistent as my mom. As I type, my astounding mother has worked for Costco's corporate office for two decades and has built up an incredible retirement account out of diligence, consistent savings, and dollar-cost averaging (I'll address DCA in Chapter Six).

Even without child support and with decades of being the primary breadwinner, she once again has handled it. She achieved financial peace amid dysfunction, dishonesty, and a late start. She took responsibility when others around her seemingly should have, either by court order or marital responsibility.

I think of those days when I worked at the wildlife center and we had to deal with raccoons. Those were the only animals that necessitated specialized cages. When I needed to tend to a wound or do a hands-on examination, one volunteer would grab the two handles on the side of the cage and pull them forward as hard as they could. That would slide the back of the cage forward, squeezing the raccoon against the front of the cage, immobilizing it so I could sedate it with a shot. It was called a "squeeze cage." Without sedation, that raccoon and all its flexibility and ferociousness would tear me apart (and a couple still did over those years). It didn't matter that it weighed just fifteen pounds, raccoons would do severe damage to anyone within an arm's length—sedation was the only way to deal with their ferocity.

I think in many ways, women are much like these raccoons. We are feisty, tenacious, persistent, adaptable, and totally determined (and adorable). When you get backed into a corner, just like my mom, you come out fighting! I have always found myself drawn to stories of amazing women facing tremendous adversity and overcoming the challenges of life, whether self-imposed or completely unexpected.

You are remarkable! No one can care for you the way you can care for you. You are your best life plan, and that's good news.

A SINGLE WOMAN CAN CHANGE THE COURSE OF THOUSANDS

Over the last few years, I have been privileged to speak to thousands of women across the nation about facing their finances head on and expecting positive change. They have all they need within themselves to change their lives for the better, enjoy the journey, and live with peace in their finances—often they just need someone to show them how.

Every time I present in front of a group, I get to bring honor to the woman who started it all for me, my wonderful mom. I thank God my mom showed me what it was to work hard, stay later, get there early, to be a great team player, and to take a risk on the one person you can count on, yourself.

My mom's financial independence did *not* happen overnight, nor did she inherit a big windfall. It was through education, hard work, and consistency. She chose to develop a new way of thinking during a period when my father and stepdad should have been fulfilling their "role" and caring for their children and being responsible. They weren't, and they didn't, but Mom didn't get bitter and wallow. She got to work.

Stop waiting for someone else to care for you and start working. You are so very capable. Don't tell yourself you can't. Be your biggest cheerleader, not your own worst critic.

PAT YOURSELF ON THE BACK, YOU DESERVE IT — THE GOOD NEWS

Since women are so fierce and determined, we have continued to permeate areas of study and lead in arenas that were once dominated by men. Finance is definitely one of them.

Statistics women should marvel in:

⌃ 51 percent of wealth is in the hands of women[4]

⌃ Women own more than eleven million businesses[5]

⌃ Women are better investors than men[6]

⌃ Women are graduating from college at a much faster rate than men, with both undergraduate and graduate degrees[7]

Maybe you're reading those statistics and saying, "Well, that is great for those ladies, but I feel more like your mom at forty-three." Take heart. Current problems are always temporary. You have been created with a purpose, and it is never too late to start rewriting your story. Don't eliminate yourself. You must invest in your education because nothing will change if you don't think differently.

Insanity is doing the same thing over and over and expecting different results.

Books from the library, online videos, and podcasts are free, and you can listen or read while getting ready for work or in your car, etc. Don't devalue the small, seemingly insignificant seed you have in your hand right now. There is so much that is right in your world. Focus on that. Water that small seed and know that things will get better, not just for you, but for the generations coming up behind you. If it's not enough for you to change for yourself, then

---

4   Wealth Track. June 28, 2019. "51% of Personal Wealth in the U.S. is Controlled by Women." https://wealth-track.com/51-percent-of-personal-wealth-in-the-u-s-is-controlled-by-women/
5   Stacy Francis. CNBC. October 21, 2019. "11 Tips for 11 Million Women—How Female Entrepreneurs Can Beat the Odds." https://www.cnbc.com/2019/10/21/how-todays-11-million-female-entrepreneurs-can-beat-the-odds.html
6   Fidelity Investments. May 18, 2019. "Who's the Better Investor: Men or Women?" https://www.fidelity.com/about-fidelity/individual-investing/better-investor-men-or-women
7   National Center for Education Statistics. Digest of Education Statistics. "Bachelor's, master's, and doctor's degrees conferred by postsecondary institutions, by sex of student and discipline division: 2016-17." https://nces.ed.gov/fastfacts/display.asp?id=72

think about the others who need you to charge ahead and show them what is possible.

Greatness and generosity lie within you, too.

You need to be ready to handle the money you have *and,* moreover, help prepare the generations to follow (daughters/sons, grandkids, and nieces/nephews) to know what to do with what they have. This isn't taught in school. You can help be a part of the solution. It starts with you and me doing our part.

> *You can't give to others what you do not have. You are blessed to be a blessing.*

MOST IMPORTANT TAKEAWAYS

1. Women are *awesome*!

2. To reinvent your life, you need to think new thoughts. Get educated.

3. Current problems are always temporary.

4. You need education about your finances, and you must pass that on to the next generation.

NEXT STEPS

1. Head to the library and check out some of the books mentioned in the back and begin consuming new thoughts every day. Consistency is key. A supertanker doesn't change direction immediately. Slow and steady wins the race.

2. Download two to three podcasts about money. Get fanatical learning new things. Find what interests you and let it wash over you.

3. Watch YouTube videos—lots of free stuff for you to fill your beautiful head with.

4. Read positive books right before bed. No TV or electronics for the last sixty minutes before bed—that's just a good, healthy habit. But also, what you put in at the end of the day is proven to give your subconscious something to "think on" all night long. Make it worthwhile brain food!

CHAPTER 4

NOT-SO-GOOD NEWS

> *Your mistakes do not define you.*
> *Neither do opinions others have*
> *based on your mistakes.*

A MAN IS NOT A PLAN

At fifteen, I thought a man would be my plan. Divorced at twenty-four, I learned my lesson the hard way. Unintentionally, I found out the same thing at thirty-two. Randy is an amazing provider, fantastic planner, incredible husband, and all-around tremendous supporter of my hopes and dreams. Still, I ignorantly waited for him to do what I needed to do for myself. I certainly love his support, and it makes the journey a lot easier when two are yoked up and heading in the same direction, but I am ultimately responsible for me.

Self-care and personal responsibility belonged to me, and they belong to you. You must captain your own financial ship, even if you are married. At the very least, you must be a well-equipped first mate on that ship who can handle the cargo and lives under your care. It makes me so proud that you have read this far because it shows that you desire to understand more clearly what you need to do to care for your own life.

Pat your wonderful self on the back! Girl, you got this!

GLARING REALITY OF IT ALL

There is so much wealth flooding into the hands of women, yet we still have a sobering reality:

- ⌃ Nearly half of couples don't know the passwords or how to find passwords for their spouses' bank, credit card, investment, or social media accounts[8]

- ⌃ 43 percent of couples don't agree on the age to retire[9]

- ⌃ 54 percent of couples don't agree on how much they need to save for retirement[10]

- ⌃ Women are living, on average, seven years longer than men[11]

- ⌃ The average life expectancy of a sixty-five-year-old woman is eighty-six[12]

- ⌃ 80 percent of men die married and 80 percent of married women die single[13]

- ⌃ The average age of widowhood is fifty-nine[14]

---

8   Fidelity Investments. 2018. "Couples & Money Study." https://www.fidelity.com/bin-public/060_www_fidelity_com/documents/pr/couples-fact-sheet.pdf
9   Ibid.
10 Ibid.
11 World Health Organization. 2019. "Female life expectancy." https://www.who.int/gho/women_and_health/mortality/situation_trends_life_expectancy/en/
12 Social Security Administration. 2020. "Benefits Planner: Life Expectancy." https://www.ssa.gov/planners/lifeexpectancy.html
13 Mary Beth Franklin. Investment News. May 23, 2019. "Dealing with Widows Requires Empathy and Patience." https://www.investmentnews.com/article/20190523/BLOG05/190529973/dealing-with-widows-requires-empathy-and-patience
14 United States Census Bureau. May 2011. "Number, Timing, and Duration of Marriages and Divorces: 2009." https://www.census.gov/prod/2011pubs/p70-125.pdf

If you are single, be thankful most of those statistics don't apply to you. But if marriage is somewhere on your horizon, please keep these in mind and make sure you are fully prepared with eyes wide open prior to your wedding date. If you are divorced, you likely felt the impact of some of those statistics from years gone by.

Women know we live longer than our male counterparts, but can you guess what the average life expectancy was for humans in the year 1900? Let's just lump men and women in the same category.

The answer: Forty-seven. Can you believe that? Forty-seven! That stat makes smoke come out of my head just trying to make sense of it. Just 120 years ago people lived, on average, just a few years longer than my current age today of forty-three. Crazy. If you were alive, you worked. Long-term retirement, as we know it, did not exist for many. Now people are living well into their eighties and beyond, which probably makes longevity the biggest risk you now face in retirement.[15]

Not market risk. Not taxes. Not inflation. Longevity. Outliving your money.

You may need to rely on your retirement savings for thirty to forty years. I am grateful we get to have so much more time to spend with those we love, doing those things that impact others and bring us joy. But being retired for thirty to forty years brings with it a host of planning factors.

Then there are other figures that adversely affect your retirement. Women are more likely to take on the burdens of childcare, even when both parents work. Daughters often bear more of the responsibility for parent care than their brothers, which means that women will spend more time out of the workforce caring for kids or parents, compared to their male counterparts.[16,] That means paying less money into Social Security or a retirement savings plan.

---

15 Centers for Disease Control and Prevention. 2010. "Table 22: Life expectancy at birth, at 65 years of age, and at 75 years of age, by race and sex: United States, selected years 1900–2007." https://www.cdc.gov/nchs/data/hus/2010/022.pdf
16 Leila Schochet. Center for American Progress. March 28, 2019. "The Child Care Crisis Is Keeping Women Out of the Workforce." https://www.americanprogress.org/issues/early-childhood/reports/2019/03/28/467488/child-care-crisis-keeping-women-workforce/

All of these care factors are a testament to how amazing and resilient women are, but they take a disproportionate financial, emotional, and health toll on women.

JUST TELL ME I NEVER HAVE TO GO BACK TO WORK

Lily attended one of my seminars in June 2008. She took me up on my offer for an initial visit at our office. When she came in to meet with me, I discovered Lily had lived through many of the not-so-good statistics that plague women across our country. Lily unofficially retired at fifty-three to care for her mom, who died four years later from complications with dementia. Lily's dad had passed away many years before. Now that Lily was in her late fifties, she didn't want to go back to work, and her husband James didn't want her to, either. James was sixty-two, enjoyed a great-paying job, and intended on working until Medicare kicked in at sixty-five. Then he was joyfully going to retire with his bride. Their big plan was to tour Europe on some of the exciting bike tours they had been reading about and get the chance to discover some little-known towns for great wine and tasty treats.

Just one month before Lily's sixtieth birthday, mere months after their thirty-fifth wedding anniversary, James passed away from a sudden heart attack. She was devastated.

Lily was living out the terrible reality so many ladies face in and approaching retirement. She was widowed with no warning. She had enjoyed many years raising their children. She also spent nearly four years of her life caring for her ailing mother. Both of those life choices took her out of the labor force, which kept her from contributing to Social Security or a 401(k) during those years.

When she came in for her visit with me, instead of just focusing on the details of her money, I wanted to focus on what truly mattered— her core values. She said she wanted security and independence, she did not want to have to go back to work, and she absolutely did not want to be a burden on her kids. She had lived that burden while taking care of her mom and didn't want to subject her children to the same hardships she faced after caring for her mother.

Probing a bit more, she told me she and James had often dreamed about traveling with the kids and grandkids on a big Disney Cruise on their dime—a once-in-a-lifetime trip. She still had many destinations she wanted to explore herself and thought she could begin to travel with some girlfriends or her sister. Those were the things that really mattered to her. Talking about that big family trip brought a smile to her face and joy back into her heart.

Even though all her financial pieces were going to need attention, we needed to start at the core of what money meant to her. That was the true starting line, and that is where it all began (Lily's story continues in Chapter Seven).

SADLY, THERE'S MORE — GRAY DIVORCE

I recall one day I had six initial visits with different gals. This day stood out more than many others because each of those women had been married at some time in their lives, and all were now divorced and single.

Somewhere between a third and a half of marriages end in divorce, depending on which source you use. It used to be the "seven-year itch," but those who have been married longer than twenty-five years are now one of the fastest-growing segments to get divorced. This is called "Gray Divorce." While some studies have shown that men fare worse emotionally following a divorce because they tend to have fewer social connections that they have sustained on their own, common sense would say that women have a more difficult time financially. Women are more likely to have dropped out of the workforce, stalling careers and putting retirement savings on hold, to care for children or aged parents; in a Gray Divorce they don't see any financial recompense for those sacrifices.

I am not at all bashing men by saying, "A man is not a plan." That is not my intention at all. I adore my husband and the incredible work he has done for women and their families over his career. I also have three amazing young men we're raising to be strong, supportive, and respectful. If they decide to get married, I want them to help care for and support their future wives, but I don't want them to be the sole key to those women's success or happiness. It's impossible to be someone's end-all-be-all. Only God is perfect. I want any future daughter-in-law to be able to adequately stand on her own, making the combined sum of her and my son much stronger than the individual parts.

Making changes within the long history of a relationship is *not* easy. I do not want to sugar-coat this. This was a monumental struggle for Randy and me for a span of years. At times as I lay crying on the floor, it felt insurmountable. By putting all the financial decision-making and know-how on Randy, I had set him up for failure. But my realizing I couldn't abdicate my personal responsibilities made Randy feel as though I didn't trust him. I was upsetting the status quo, and had to admit that this cycle was partly because I didn't trust *me*. Let me say again, *it was really hard*, but *so worth it*. Quitting would have been easier in the beginning, but vastly more costly in the end. The struggle and arguments are worth the understanding and connectedness that comes later.

If you are facing some of these issues due to financial problems/concerns/difficulties, get educated and hire a financial adviser you both like to act as your money therapist. As hard as it was to realize that I was the problem, it was empowering to know that I was also the solution. The same can be true of you.

Come on, Wonder Woman, you've got this handled!

IRRESPONSIBILITY AND IGNORANCE DON'T PAY YOUR BILLS

You could be placing your trust in a man, a woman, inheritance from your parents, or the government. Trust isn't bad. It's healthy to have. But all those sources can let you down if you wield trust blindly. We are all broken and faulty people, and we cannot be the sole source for anyone's joy or success, nor should we place that full responsibility on someone else; that's irresponsible.

My desire is for you to understand what you have, know where your money is, and know how to make it all function optimally. Life can change in an instant. You need to have a clear plan. Let's make one and walk this wonderful road of life together.

Are you with me?! Throw on your stilettos, cross-trainers, or hiking boots, and let's get walking!

> *You are responsible for your life, no one else.*

MOST IMPORTANT TAKEAWAYS

1. A man is not a plan—you are *not* a victim of your circumstances, you are a victor!

2. Longevity (outliving your money) may be the biggest risk you face in retirement.

3. Couples need to get on the same page about money and retirement.

4. You will likely be the last woman standing—80 percent of women die single.

5. Caring for parents or kids puts you "a leg down" financially.

6. Divorce often financially affects women more so than men.

NEXT STEPS

1. Determine today that you—and no one else—are in control of your finances—YOU ARE THE PLAN.

2. Take your partner to a neutral place like a coffee shop (or maybe somewhere with stronger drinks like a winery or brewery…haha) and have a candid conversation with them about money values. Whatever it takes, start the dialog. Don't let fear or differences stop you from having these discussions.

3. Keep reading and studying. Your education on this topic is paramount—your BEST LIFE depends on it (on you).

CHAPTER 5

YOU NEED A PLAN

> *Execution is a critical element toward becoming great.*

HE WAS THE BRAINS AND I WAS THE BRAWN

"You need to talk to your financial adviser," were the words scribbled on a piece of torn yellow legal pad paper. Lorna had just arrived at our office to pick up her taxes and handed us this ominous scrawled note. Up to this moment, we had never met Lorna, only her husband, Ron. They were tax clients of the CPA who shares our office. Many couples, like Ron and Lorna, have one person who handles the preparation of the return. That wasn't unusual, but Lorna's situation was.

Lorna contacted us, via email, about one month before April 15th to tell us her husband was ill. Just a couple of weeks later, he passed away, so she had come in that day to pick up her taxes. After the door opened, it shut behind two women. One was Lorna and the other woman was a girlfriend of hers. With her friend's help, we found out for the first time: Lorna was deaf.

Lorna was married forty-six years to the love of her life. They met as teens. He had polio as a child. "He was the brains, and I was the brawn," she said. She meant he handled all the finances and the "thinking stuff," and she handled all the physical labor in the house and their lives. Within a short period, it became apparent this would turn out to be the most extreme case I'd ever seen of somebody detached from their finances. She knew how to write a check and knew where they banked, but that was it. Lorna and Ron had no children. She had a brother in Chicago, but even the friend she brought for "moral support" wasn't overly close to her.

Lorna was utterly and frighteningly alone and extraordinarily vulnerable.

The wrinkled, yellow piece of paper was written by her attorney: "You need to talk to your financial adviser."

She handed it to me and asked if we could help her—although she was deaf, she could respond verbally. This moment started the clock on our deep dive over the next eight weeks. We had six appointments, two more than our typical new client process, because the communication barrier obviously created a few challenges.

Randy came up with a great plan. Instead of us writing back and forth on a piece of paper to communicate, we would use the talk-to-text functions on our phones and tablets to communicate our ideas to her. Genius! But we couldn't just pick up the phone and do a conference call with her investment companies to order forms, make changes, etc. With a deaf client, we needed to improvise.

Our first visit was revealing. Lorna didn't know what an IRA or brokerage account was and didn't know if they had life insurance or a pension. At the end of the first visit, we grabbed samples of different statements—life insurance, annuities, brokerage accounts, IRAs, and others—saying, "Lorna, take these home and try and find something that looks like this!" On her second visit, she brought in a stack of papers more than a foot high, some of it more than twenty years old, with that musty smell of aging paper and ink. We began filtering through it and figuring out what was current and if it had anything to do with their financial picture. It was tedious investigative work, but every visit ended the same way. She would have tears in her eyes (and so would we) as she gave us big hugs.

I'll never forget the day Lorna looked across the table and bluntly said, "Arwen, am I going to be broke?" This is the greatest fear many retirees face, particularly after 2008. It's gut-wrenching to discuss the fear of running out of money, but it's an unfortunate reality for many women who experience poverty after the death of their spouse. [17]

We did for her exactly what we do for all those who sit at our table. We did our best to take all the financial items she owned, along with pension and Social Security, and plug them into our retirement calculator to generate a clear picture of how it might all work together, or what we might need to reposition. I always say to any prospective client that the second visit is by far the very best, most eye-opening visit we have with anyone. That visit comes before anyone ever becomes a client. Whether you become a client of ours or not doesn't matter in the big picture. What matters is that we always strive to leave you better than we found you. To show you how all the parts of your financial life can work in concert with one another. The process is designed to provide the clarity and direction everyone needs to be able to take the next step.

Lorna needed such clarity and direction.

Ultimately, Lorna decided to move back to Chicago to be near her brother and family and have a bigger support system around her. She felt it was best to work with an adviser closer to her there and also have her brother's help, and we agreed that was the best choice for her since advising remotely with a deaf client posed greater difficulty.

---

17 T. Ghilarducci, M.S. Jaimes, & A. Webb. Schwartz Center for Economic Policy Analysis and Department of Economics, The New School for Social Research, Policy Note Series. 2018. "Old-Age Poverty: Single Women & Widows & a Lack of Retirement Security." https://www.economicpolicyresearch.org/images/Retirement_Project/Single-Women-Widows-PN-edited-12.21-final.pdf

We happily parted ways with hugs, more tears, and a woman determined to face the next season of her retirement.

This is why you need to have a clear plan that is comprehensive and easy to understand. Do not delay; start now. This applies if you are married or single, because someone will always need to come behind you and pick up the pieces following your death, be it a spouse, significant other, kids, or grandkids. Please make it easier on yourself and those you cherish.

TIME FOR A PLAN, BUT WHERE TO START?

We're going to begin with a little bit of inventory. Before you ignore this—I know, it's a little bit of work—remember this is where real change begins. We're not going to dive too deep or be exhaustive, but this baby step can be the difference in starting on the right financial path. You need this—all your worrying and embarrassment and frustration won't change things. Taking action will.

We're going to do a basic financial inventory. Grab a pencil and begin to jot down anything you know about these items below. Dog-ear this page. Write directly on this page—circle, star, or highlight anything of question—and bring it to your adviser. If it doesn't apply, skip it, but if you are unsure, make a note to get some direction when you sit down with your financial adviser.

+ Social Security value at full retirement age (FRA)
+ Pensions: PERS, TRS, company-sponsored
+ Rental income / real estate
+ Individual Retirement Accounts (IRAs)
+ Roth IRAs
+ Company plans: 401(k), 403(b), 401(a), 457, TSP…
+ Solo 401(k), SEP-IRA…
+ Brokerage accounts
+ Annuity contracts: variable, fixed, indexed, immediate

+ Life insurance: whole, IUL, universal, term
+ Long-term care policy
+ Certificates of deposit
+ Money markets
+ Checking and savings
+ Any other policies or accounts with any value?

SORRY, BUT HIS EX-WIFE ACCIDENTALLY GOT YOUR INHERITANCE

Our eighty-five-year old client brought in her new husband. She had been a client of ours for several years, but after being widowed, she rekindled a relationship with a gentleman she knew over the past forty years. He hadn't had a financial adviser, but after three years of marriage to our client, he liked the care and service his new bride was receiving from us and decided to meet with me to see if we could improve his situation.

As Ida and Gordon sat together, determining that they were wanting to start combining their finances, Gordon spoke about his 401(k) from Boeing and a trust he had for his kids with his ex-wife. He had been divorced now for many years, and his priorities were taking care of Ida and leaving a legacy to his children. As I asked more questions, I determined that he retired from Boeing in 1993, but never rolled his Boeing company plan out into an Individual Retirement Account (IRA).

"Gordon, why didn't you roll your 401(k) from Boeing into an IRA once you left?" His response, "I didn't know I could."

Wow. I couldn't believe twenty-five years had passed, and he didn't know that he could or *should* have rolled his qualified plan out of Boeing into an IRA.

That was very surprising.

So, here's the deal, my good women. If you worked at a company where you had a 401(k), 403(b), TSP, or some type of retirement plan, and you no longer work for that company, you have the option to transition that money into a self-directed Individual Retirement Account, or IRA. There are many reasons for doing so, primary of which is control. Make sure to get some direction, but often it's most prudent to "roll over" funds from a former employer into your IRA, so you can dictate where to invest it, have many more investment choices, and keep your beneficiaries up to date. This is allowed under the IRS code, so it is not a taxable event if you do it correctly. Do it wrong and that could be a different story, so make sure you are getting help to do it right. There are also significant benefits from consolidation, simplification, and future tax planning and reporting.

"You know, Arwen, I tried calling Boeing a month ago to do an address change, and I was on hold for thirty-five minutes. I got irritated, so I hung up!" Gordon told us one day.

"I totally understand, Gordon. We have to be on hold with companies all the time. Boeing is one of them. I know how frustrating it can be. We would be happy to help you with your address change, but I have one question for you. You have had that account at Boeing for a very long time. Who is the beneficiary listed on it?"

Gasp.

Gordon glanced over at his new wife, paused for what seemed like an eternity, then finally choked out a response. "Oh gosh," he said. "I need to get that changed. I think it's still my ex-wife."

Yikes! His ex-wife! Geez.

This happens more times than you would like to think. When you fail to transition your old company retirement plans to an IRA under your own care and watchful eye, you could give up all control on how that money is managed and invested. You have limited accessibility. The company can decide to change the provider from Vanguard to Fidelity, and if similar investments aren't available, they can just liquidate the entire account and throw it into a cash account, making a "point nothing" rate of return, all without asking your permission.

Moreover, employer-sponsored plans like 401(k)s are required to withhold a mandatory 20 percent tax on distributions (what you pull out), often more than you need to cover the tax bill. Additionally, it complicates matters when you need to start taking your Required Minimum Distributions (Chapter Eight), putting greater responsibility (and chance of making a mistake) on you.

Finally, people often forget to update beneficiaries with new spouses or grandkids, just like Gordon did. So, knowing what you have and who's listed as a beneficiary is vitally important to those you love and care for.

NO MICRO-CLIMATES

So, now you have begun to organize yourself (hopefully on paper, as I asked, not just in your head) and have a clear idea of what you own. You've identified what matters most to you, and your values. You are now thinking plainly about all the items that make up your financial life. But the perplexing question you most likely have is, "How do all these financial pieces I have work together to pay my bills for the rest of my life, pay for future health care, *and* let me have fun, too?" (Okay, so maybe you don't ask it that way, but that is certainly what you're thinking.)

The issue a lot of ladies face is they unintentionally plan within "micro-climates."

My zoology background brings me to this analogy. The world over, you have micro-climates such as the temperate climate, polar climate, tundra, tropics, desert, arid, etc. Each is relatively self-contained, and the specific plants and animals that thrive in each micro-climate have different needs—if you pull an animal from the tundra and put them in the desert, often the result is death.

People often make financial decisions in micro-climates. You want to determine the options for your Social Security, so you reluctantly march into the Social Security office, get that info and decide on that matter. Then you talk to your CPA or accountant about your tax issues and make plans accordingly. Then you speak to the pension provider regarding how you should take your pension, what sounds best, and make an irrevocable decision. Then you talk to somebody about your health care or long-term care needs, next Medicare, and then you speak with your broker or financial adviser about your at-risk assets in your investment account.

Those are all micro-climates. You're treating them as though they function alone.

Yet, as anyone in life sciences can explain, the micro-climates don't actually operate in a vacuum. Like an invasive species or a hole in the ozone layer, the micro-climates have to operate complementarily to each other, or the whole system could be put out of balance. Your retirement is like the whole-earth view—massive pollution in one area may cause foul weather in another. If you don't have a strategy for how your big picture will act in a Great-Recession-like event, then even fantastic planning in each separate area individually may not be sufficient or best.

Micro-climate mentality is one of the most common issues we see on first appointments with people in our office. They plan these areas separately. They may have made huge, sometimes irrevocable, decisions within these micro-climates instead of making their decisions based on an inclusive and comprehensive plan that has all matters considered. We call this our *Best Life Retirement Plan*. It's so incredible when you see how each piece of your financial puzzle functions *and* determine how it works within the bigger picture. Some prominent elements include when to begin Social Security or pension payments, or on what date you can confidently retire once and for all!

IT'S NOT THE BATHROOM OR THE ESCALATOR
THAT IS MOST IMPORTANT TO LOCATE FIRST

You've arrived at the mall. You have a few places you want to go, but your first stop is the Sunglass Hut. You scan the directory, find the category of accessories, follow your pointer finger down A, D…S, Sa…Su…ah ha, the Sunglass Hut: 242. You turn your gaze back to the layout of the mall in front of you, scanning the wings and floors, finally locating the Sunglass Hut. Found it!

Now you're on your way!

Or are you?

To determine how to get there, you must locate the red dot indicating "YOU ARE HERE."

This baseline plan or YOU ARE HERE initial scenario is the essential step one of planning where you'd like to go. You can't estimate how much money or coverage you might have in the future without knowing what you currently have.

I hope you wouldn't go into an appointment with a new doctor and begin with a list of the prescriptions you want them to write before they have completed a basic exam. If a doctor didn't perform a thorough examination to determine your baseline medical condition and ask about medications and allergies and review prior medical records, they could lose their license by prescribing something that could harm you. That's malpractice.

A couple of years ago we bought another financial professional's business. He wasn't a fiduciary, meaning a professional who is required to operate in his clients' best interests. He only offered life insurance, long-term care insurance, and annuities. This isn't to say he was acting poorly, just to explain that he had a limited range of tools to use with his clients.

We sat with his former clients to show them how their investments worked together and built a comprehensive *Best Life Retirement Plan*. Once these clients could fully visualize their current financial landscape, in its entirety, many of them got upset at their former representative because of some of the financial tools they owned. They questioned why they owned something they didn't need, the quantities of some holdings, and worse yet, why they were paying fees for something that didn't benefit them.

By themselves, the products they had weren't bad. We often use these same tools in many of our clients' plans. What was problematic was when the tools were applied and to whom.

The same principle for physicians and doctors applies to giving financial and retirement advice. Telling you how to invest your current 401(k), what stocks you should buy, or when to take your pension or Social Security could be highly irresponsible and could constitute something like "financial malpractice" if I am not looking at all the parts of your financial life and how they could be affected by these decisions.

If you're working with someone who is planning in a micro-climate, they may be duplicating investments you already have or neglecting an area where you need more coverage. Additionally, I wouldn't be acting in my fiduciary capacity and doing what is in your best interest if I gave you advice without having enough information. Every investment must have a purpose and be prescribed at the appropriate time, in the proper dosage for your unique situation.

A comprehensive approach is vital to your overall financial health and longevity.

We determine this YOU ARE HERE baseline in our second visit after our team has had time to gather and input all your financial information. Although this visit is before a person formally engages us as their adviser, I believe this is the most valuable visit we have with anyone we sit with. At this point, we have a broad picture of their values, and we can run through many scenarios to consider things like Social Security timing and how to defend against a recession, time a mortgage payoff, or figure out a travel budget for the next ten years.

Determining this baseline is so much fun when we can move that YOU ARE HERE sticker to some sweet travel destination—Bora Bora or Mexico, perhaps?

Identifying where in the world you are is critical. You don't want to make any changes to your current picture until you know exactly where you stand today. Right? Neither do I!

Don't make decisions based on the partial view of your current picture. No micro-climates, my wonderful friend—be sure to complete the checklist earlier in this chapter to help get you started.

> *It takes faith to believe in something better, yet you must put in the work. One can't exist without the other.*

MOST IMPORTANT TAKEAWAYS

1. Do not delay in getting an idea of what you have.

2. When you no longer work for a company (separate from service), you may want to consider rolling your company plan into an Individual Retirement Account (IRA) to keep greater control over your money and investment choices.

3. Make sure your beneficiaries and your mailing address stay up to date.

4. Avoid micro-climates within your financial world.

NEXT STEPS

1. Complete the basic inventory questions in this chapter before moving to the next chapter.

2. If you no longer work for a company, and you still have money there in a company plan of some kind, get help from an adviser to consider opening up an IRA and rolling it over to retain greater control of your assets. You can combine multiple old company plans into one IRA. No need for multiple IRAs.

3. Meet with a fiduciary retirement planner who has the tools to help you combine all that you own in a single picture to help you make the right decisions about your money and future. Start interviewing individuals within the next six weeks. Don't let momentum get away. Meet with two or three or more to find a great fit. Many planners will do this for free, like our firm, but some will charge a fee, so make sure you know that upfront. Your self-imposed deadline to have a first meeting with someone: ____/____/20____

CHAPTER 6

INCOME FOR LIFE

> *It's always easier to go quietly*
> *than to put up a fight.*
> *You were never built for easy.*

LET'S MAKE A DEAL!

"These people, dressed as they are, come from all over the United States to make deals at the Marketplace of America! Let's Make a Deal! And here is TV's top big dealer, Monty Hall!" (Clapping).

I loved that show as a little girl. They'd call Sally, and she would jump out of her chair, screaming, dressed as a clown, bumblebee, or cowgirl. Arms flailing, she'd land beside Monty and side hug him, jumping up and down as he made small talk. I often imagine a Monty-Hall-style game show for the newly retired.

"Welcome, Sally, where are you from?"

In a slight southern drawl: "Well, Monty, I am originally from Savannah, Georgia, but now I live near my grandkids in Boise, Idaho!" she responds in an overly excited voice.

"That's great! So, you love being with your grandkids?"

"More than anything! And when I retire from nursing next year, I will get to be with them more often!"

"Well, that's great! Okay, let's see what possible retirement options might lie behind door number one, two, or three."

The announcer's voice comes on over the speakers and begins to reveal the great options that could lie behind two of those doors. "Well Sally, behind one of these doors lies a retirement full of dreams, vacations, no money worries, and memory upon memory with your grandkids. It is full of peace, security, and life! You will never have to worry about being a burden on your kids or having enough money if you need nursing home coverage, AND you will have the opportunity to leave money to all six of your grandkids and your three children!"

"Oooooh!" The crowd responds with applause as Sally looks excitedly at the host and many of the audience members. "Or, maybe you get a new motorhome!" The crowd erupts as a brand new, class A, thirty-six-foot motorhome is revealed, fully loaded with four slide-outs, valued at over $300,000.

That leaves the final option: the booby prize.

"All right, Sally, which door do you choose? Door number one, door number two, or door number three?" The crowd begins to shout at Sally which door they think has the best option behind it.

"I really want that secure and peaceful retirement. I am going to pick door number three."

"All right, please reveal what is behind door number three!"

After a long, nerve-wracking pause from the announcer..."It's a brand-new motorhome!" The crowd erupts in excitement as Sally jumps up and down, then obviously begins to struggle over whether she takes the motorhome or risks getting the booby prize.

"Well, Monty, I really love that motorhome, but, being a widow, I really can't see myself doing that kind of travel alone, and that's a lot to take care of for one person, so I am going to take my chance to see what is behind door number one!"

"All right, Sally. So, you give up the $300,000 motorhome for the hope of a peaceful retirement. Let's see…did you win that? Reveal what is behind door number one!"

As the door opens, there is big piggy bank with a check for $750,000 on the table. A big sign above it reads, "BROKE AT EIGHTY-FIVE." Sally hears the dreaded sound of failure. "Womp-womp-woooooooooomp." The crowd seems confused as to why that is the booby prize, and so does Sally.

"Ooooh, I am so sorry, Sally, but let's see what is behind door number two." The door slides open, revealing the same piggy bank with only $250,000 in it, but the sign above it reads, "PEACEFUL RETIREMENT, $1.1 MILLION AT NINETY."

Huh? How could that be? If she starts out with three times more money, how could she be broke at eighty-five, yet have $1 million if she retires with only $250,000?

SIMPLE MATHEMATICS

People often listen to their friends, commercials, or other outside information about how much money they need to have saved when they retire. Yes, that amount is a vital consideration, but it is *not* the most important.

The two most important components that outweigh how much you've saved for retirement are *income* and *expenses*. Period. It's all about cash flow!

I had back-to-back visits one day that felt very much like the scenario I've outlined for the fictitious Sally. One couple came in who, when they were each sixty-five, planned to retire from a local hospital. They were both registered nurses who had put in seventy-five years, collectively, and were retiring with $250,000 saved in their retirement plans. They each had healthy pensions and Social Security benefits. They were entirely debt free and owned (free and clear) a three-bedroom, two-bath home worth $450,000, so their monthly living expenses were about $4,500 per month.

In contrast, the other couple was a similar age but had $2 million in retirement savings and no pensions. They each had Social Security benefits, yet owned a $1.9 million home with a $400,000 mortgage and a lifestyle that cost them $11,000 per month.

	COUPLE #1 – $250K IN RET.	COUPLE #2 – $2M IN RET.
Social Security (His)	$2,550	$2,550
Social Security (Hers)	$2,550	$1,800
Pension (His)	$3,100	0
Pension (Hers)	$3,300	0
Monthly Expenses	$4,500	$11,000
Money needed from Ret. Accts. (after removing 20% taxes from income)	Monthly cash flow NONE - had +$4,700 extra every month	Monthly cash flow -$7,520
Money at age 90	$1.5 million	Broke at 85

Make sense? It's simple mathematics.

Women routinely make assumptions that they need more than $250,000 or $500,000 to retire. The "big-media" messaging supports that myth. We see that blown out of the water all the time. I have seen women who have started over at fifty with the death of a spouse or a divorce. A woman in this scenario may come in with $100,000 in retirement savings in her late sixties, but she has done so many other things right. She keeps expenses low, is mortgage-free, maybe enjoys some rental income (or a paying roommate), or works for a government, school, or hospital, where pensions still exist. She is on a path to a beautiful, restful, relaxing retirement.

It's all about income overlaid with expenses.

Therefore, seeing everything you have integrated into a comprehensive plan like our *Best Life Retirement Plan* is critical to your overall retirement. Don't be fooled by the "big number" of retirement savings you *think* you need. It's essential that you have a complete income plan that shows how much money you need, month after month, year after year. Get the facts.

Recall 80 percent of married men die married, so if you are married now, the likelihood is high that your spouse could die before you both *truly* see if the plan worked or not. Yet 73 percent of couples disagree as to whether they have a retirement income plan created.[18]

This bears repeating—73 percent disagree.

It's black or white…you either do or you don't.

Handling this money piece is imperative to your future of peace and certainty. You need an understandable document that shows how much money you need, month after month, year after year, and what your *income gap* could be.

MIND THE GAP

In 2016, Randy and I co-wrote a *Forbes* article called "Mind the Gap—In Retirement." In London when you ride the Tube (public transit railway), there are signs all over that say, "Mind the Gap," meaning the gap between the platform and the train. We often use that expression for this part of retirement planning. If your monthly income is $1,200 short (income gap), then you must focus your energy to "Mind the Gap" about what you're going to do to make sure that you have $1,200 coming in from your retirement accounts.

During working years, you focus on work, saving, raising children, volunteering, just doing life. In the background, you accumulate a retirement nest egg, often on autopilot. You contribute a piece of each paycheck to your 401(k) and IRAs without giving it much thought until you near retirement age. The fact of the matter is, when you reach retirement, all of that background work

---

18 Fidelity Investments. 2011. "Couples Retirement Study." https://www.fidelity.com/bin-public/060_www_fidelity_com/documents/pr/couples-fact-sheet.pdf

immediately comes to the foreground. It's sort of staring you square in your face, taunting you, like Goliath, ready to fight.

You can't help but look at your retirement account and say, "Well, I guess this is it. This is what I have to last for the rest of my life." Psychologically, that's a big shift for women. Still, if you don't get the "money part" out of the way, then you could spend hours, days, and weeks of this precious time of your life concentrating on the money and trying to figure out how to beat an opponent bigger and more formidable than you. The giant looms large to defeat you, and you are just now stepping into the fight with a few small stones and a slingshot. Yikes.

Hope you have a great coach and God on your side.

In my experience, this is the main challenge that most women face—income planning. This is a massive undertaking for the untrained. How do you go from those years where you have money coming in month after month, to suddenly not working? There's a big drop in earned income. Maybe you haven't started Social Security, either. Maybe you're not fortunate enough to have a pension.

Or maybe you are prepared and just don't know it yet. Your opponent may be bigger, but they are slow and sluggish. With some great coaching and direction, nimble movements, and faith added to your effort, you can make Goliath fall. We help women do this all the time. You can do this!

So, where do you get the income from? Let's look at some of your income options.

INHERITANCE ISN'T A GOOD FINANCIAL PLAN

You head to the Midwest to celebrate Christmas with your mom. She's now in her eighties. You dispense with hugs at the door and then ask, "Mom, how are you feeling?" She responds with a spring in her step, "Great, Honey. Thanks for asking!" Perhaps you feel overcome with disappointment.

That's not good. Really, not good at all.

An estimated $30 trillion will be passed via inheritance over the next twenty years.[19] Some of that may fall your way, but you need to have a plan that can function without it, so keep lovin' on Mom and valuing all the days she is around.

THE OTHER GUYS

"What sources of income do you have?" In our first conversation with you, this is a question we always ask. This conversation is vital to all the future planning you will be doing.

We commonly see 1) Part-Time Wages, 2) Social Security, 3) Pension, and 4) Rental Income. You may be asking, what about RMDs, my annuity payments, or dividends from my investment accounts? Those are the retirement assets that help bridge the gap, and we'll dive into them later on, but they are not sources of income as it relates to the income planning discussion we are currently having.

Part-Time Wages: One gal worked twenty-two years for Microsoft, and when she came in for her second visit, she had been fired. Those wages were a huge part of the planning process and were instantly eliminated. She said, "If I can stay retired, let's do it, but if I need to go back to work for a few years to make the retirement picture pristine, please let me know." At fifty-five, the retirement plan would barely sustain her and her spouse through their nineties, and left a lot of "what ifs" without solid coverage, so being fully retired was not the best option.

---

19   MacKenzie Sigalos. CNBC. July 10, 2018. "$30 Trillion Is About to Change Hands in the U.S." https://www.cnbc.com/2018/06/28/wealth-transfer-baby-boomers-estate-heir-inheritance.html

> **WHY PLAN TO 100?**
>
> Life expectancies continue to climb, with centenarians being one of the—maybe even *the*—fastest-growing age groups in the world.[20] With those sorts of statistics, even though our grandparents and parents may have only lived to their seventies or eighties, we think we should prepare to be some of those who live to 100. If you plan to live that long and don't, you may end up leaving an inheritance for your loved ones. But if you don't plan to live that long and you *do,* it could drastically change your financial picture and lifestyle. So, particularly for women, who are more likely to live longer than their spouses, we build a *Best Life Retirement Plan* to last to 100.

When she got through the intricate details of her plan, it was apparent she needed to get a job. So, she followed her passion as a photographer, setting up gigs and generating money doing what she loved.

She thought outside of the box and handled it.

Social Security: Social Security started in 1935 to care for the aging population and was viewed as an entitlement of sorts, so it was not taxed. Upon its creation, Social Security turned on at age sixty-five. That was when you started receiving your benefits. What is crazy, though, is life expectancy for people in 1935 was sixty-two! Social Security was never designed to support people living well into their eighties and nineties. That's why retirement income planning is imperative, because Social Security probably won't be enough to cover your income gap once you stop working.

---

20   Boston university School of Medicine. May 9, 2020. "New England Centenarian Study: Why Study Centenarians? An Overview." https://www.bumc.bu.edu/centenarian/overview/

Here are some of the basics you ought to know about Social Security:

- ▲ Social Security has thousands of core rules, including numerous complex formulas for couples.

- ▲ Social Security does not send out benefit statements any longer (if you are under the age of sixty). You need to go to www.ssa.gov and create a 'My SSA' account to print out your benefit statement.

- ▲ Social Security is not intended to represent your total or even a majority of your income in retirement.

- ▲ If you are currently divorced (and you haven't remarried) and you were married more than ten years, you have the option to collect against your ex-spouse's benefits. There are multiple rules behind this, but this is a planning option you don't want to ignore.[21]

Social Security is an area in which I see a lot of people planning in a micro-climate. A lot of individuals I sit with say, "I'm going to delay my Social Security, because it's more money." Or "I got laid off from my job at sixty-two. I am going to collect early." Don't rush into either of those choices, because when you make that decision it is relatively irrevocable: If you change your mind, you can pay it all back within the first twelve months, but otherwise when that choice is made, it's made. The question is, what is the best choice in the context of my entire plan and for the rest of my life?

The front page of your Social Security benefits form has a value, and that value is your full retirement age (FRA). For the ladies I currently am sitting down with, full retirement age is going to be somewhere between sixty-six and sixty-seven. Full retirement age

---

21 Social Security Administration. Benefits Planner: Retirement: If You Are Divorced. 2019. https://www.ssa.gov/planners/retire/divspouse.html#targetText=If%20your%20ex%2Dspouse%20has,pay%20the%20retirement%20benefit%20first.

represents 100 percent of your FRA value. Every year you delay that benefit, up to age seventy, your benefit increases by another 8 percent. That would mean at age seventy your benefit could exceed your FRA amount by 32 percent.

A lot of people automatically delay so they receive the larger benefit. There isn't anything inherently wrong with that thought process. However, that is not always the best decision in the long term. Sometimes there are health issues that make taking Social Security earlier a better choice. Or, maybe you get laid off from work at sixty-three and can't wait for that additional income to turn on at seventy.

Or sometimes, and I love this, we look at Social Security within the context of your retirement plan, and it's so *healthy,* we can talk about taking Social Security early. Your plan doesn't rely on Social Security to function optimally. Imagine if you received an extra $2,050 every single month for the next four years, because you took Social Security at sixty-six instead of seventy? I bet you could figure out something fun to do with it!

Something fulfilling. Something that makes others' lives better.

Maybe travel more, take the grandkids somewhere cool, fly first class occasionally, or maybe just give it away. How sweet would that be! Anything is more fun than just allowing the government to hang on to it for no specific reason.

People don't know what they don't know. They just assume delaying is the best way, but they haven't done adequate research. Seeing how Social Security functions *optimally,* within your overall plan, is a huge part of the planning process.

BRING YOUR PATIENCE AND YOUR HEADPHONES INTO THE SOCIAL SECURITY OFFICE

It is necessary to get all your possible options from the Social Security Administration, so make it a priority to go in and discover all the options you have. Take a great book or headphones to listen to music or a podcast, a large dose of patience for the wait, and get all the facts you need to make a wise decision. This is really the best way to determine your options.

One Social Security office administrator told a gal that they didn't know anything about collecting benefits on an ex-husband's Social Security. That bad information from a new and uneducated Social Security employee cost the woman $1,500 per month for *two years*. That's $36,000!

I told her to march back in there and get her benefit, to handle it. She did. But of course, Social Security won't be paying missed back pay for that mistake, so it's important to get all the facts and talk it over with your retirement planner.

If you have heard information from trusted outside sources and are not getting the same information from the clerk at the Social Security Administration (SSA), ask for someone else and dig a bit further. Get a second opinion and further confirmation.

We love helping our clients make the most of their benefits from Social Security, a program they have paid into their entire working careers.

BIGGER ISN'T ALWAYS BETTER

Pension: "Joe, do you have any survivor benefits on your $3,500 pension from Hanford?" Joe looked at me, a bit puzzled. "What do you mean?" "Well," I responded, "if you were to die tomorrow, how much money would Cathy receive from Hanford for the rest of *her* life?"

There was a very long pause. He glanced down at his wringing hands on the table, then back across at me.

"Nothing."

You could see the distress on his face; he and Cathy had clearly never had the decision posed to them that way. "Why is that?" I inquired of them both. After a moment of stunned silence, they looked at each other and then back at me. "We just thought it was best to pick the largest amount. No one gave us any reason to do otherwise."

The biggest number isn't always the best number.

If this sixty-five-year-old man, who was married to a healthy sixty-year-old triathlete, were to die unexpectedly or prematurely, that $3,500 of monthly pension income would be eliminated instantly. She could easily outlive him by fifteen to twenty years. They were debt-free and their monthly expenses totaled about $4,000, which is a very reasonable lifestyle for where they lived in the Tri-Cities area of Washington State. The pension currently met 85 percent of their income need, and on his death, that plus the smaller of the couples' Social Security benefits would be eliminated.

In dollars and cents, combining his pension and the lost Social Security, his death would mean a loss of $5,300 per month for his wife. She realized that 100 percent of her newly created "income gap" would be pulled from whatever retirement assets they had saved. It would be her prayer that between those assets and the remaining $2,700 in Social Security, she would have enough to survive for possibly another twenty-plus years.

That was a very unnecessary gamble.

We see individuals and couples making this mistake all the time. They determine their pension payout in a micro-climate, speaking about this portion of their retirement plan to the pension provider and making decisions that are often irrevocable and vitally important. They should have known *first* how that decision would affect the entire picture that spans both their lifetimes, not just what gave them the biggest number now.

Instant gratification versus long-term responsibility.

This is not to say that this couple, or others like them, was irresponsible. Quite often, it's the contrary. But without proper advice from a financial retirement planner who understands how that momentary decision progresses through a potentially lengthy retirement, people can make disastrous choices. You never want to make that decision unless you know how it will perform in *all* circumstances.

NO BRINGING BACK THE DODO BIRD

Pensions, as we now know, are going the way of the Dodo bird. Extinct.

Most private companies no longer offer them, and some of those that still do are in danger of defaulting on their obligation after decades of underfunding them.[22] Pensions are expensive to maintain, cut into the "almighty profits," and reflect long-term liabilities on a company's balance sheet.

With pensions vanishing, the past responsibility of generating guaranteed *lifetime* income managed by professionals with decades of experience has been transferred to you, the individual, with your 401(k) assets and all that financial training of yours (ha-ha-ha).

Thankfully for Joe and Cathy, their decision on Joe's pension dispersal wasn't disastrous. Cathy would have still been able to handle it financially.

We looked at all the possible "what-if" scenarios. What if they went through the worst ten years in stock market history, like 2000 through 2009? What if he died in the next ten years? What if he needed some form of nursing home care and drained a large portion of their assets, and then died, eliminating the pension and the smaller of the two Social Security checks? How would all these unknowns affect her or him?

You must play this game of "what if" prior to making decisions on collecting your pension. That is always the most effective way to make the best choice.

---

22 Alessandra Malito. MarketWatch. December 11, 2018. "The Truth About Pensions: They Aren't Dead, But Some Are Barely Holding On." https://www.marketwatch.com/story/the-truth-about-pensions-they-arent-dead-but-some-are-barely-holding-on-2018-12-11

RENTAL INCOME — HOUSE RICH AND CASH POOR

Rental Income: "My mom continually says to me, 'Honey, you're always broke.'" This was a statement coming from an eighty-five-year-old mom to her sixty-two-year-old daughter who owned six rental houses. This gal loved her rentals, enjoyed tinkering on them, and maintained a steady cash flow she received from them. On many occasions, however, one or two rentals were empty for a period. As a result, income fell short and she found herself strapped for cash.

She was house rich and cash poor.

It was a simple fix: Sell one of the rentals, pour that $300,000 into her retirement and *POOF*, no more cashflow issues. Yet her emotional attachment to her rentals stopped her from having that peace of mind. She refused to take that advice and was instead living a life of "barely getting by."

Not all our clients have rentals. For those who do, rentals can be a great source of income throughout retirement. We do, however, see that often our clients entering their seventies are focused more on simplification and consolidation than they were in their sixties. They often consider selling some or all rentals to end the frustration that comes from owning rental homes and the problems associated with tenants.

I doubt you bought a rental years ago so you would have it for the rest of your life. Be willing to detach yourself from that asset if the time is right and you get good advice to do so. The process of selling a rental is vitally important to see in the context of the entire plan. You need to know where you currently stand, and then build out another retirement scenario that shows the elimination of the rental income (and its expenses). Don't forget to incorporate the influx of cash into your overall retirement.

It can be a simple and beautiful thing.

EIGHTY-TWO AND BROKE

I recall sitting with an eighty-two-year-old widow whose daughter was a client of ours. When we sat down with her, she was frazzled and exhausted. She and her husband had built an $8.2 million net worth, primarily using rentals. Her husband died a few years ago, and she was now finding it tough to care for the multiple apartment buildings and individual rental homes she owned around the Puget Sound area. The year before, she had to borrow money from our client (her daughter) to pay her tax bill due to a lack of cash flow.

Net worth of $8.2 million but can't pay her bills. Yikes—that's just not right.

This was another situation where the sale of just one of her properties would eliminate the cash flow crunch, but she was too emotionally tied to the rentals and the connection they had to her late husband. Even more frustrating, her children had made it clear they didn't want to inherit the rentals (or the headaches) from their parents.

We own multiple rentals and love having the cash flow and growing assets. However, you can't spend them when money gets tight. House rich and cash poor doesn't put food on the table or clothes on your back. It sure doesn't help you sleep well at night, either.

This is not the plan for a peaceful or confident retirement, nor do you want to leave a legacy that maddens your heirs instead of blessing them. Many clients of ours have truly enjoyed owning rentals and have benefited from them for their retirements, but often their kids do not want to take over the management. Such factors can make rental properties challenging and costly to manage.

We want you to be able to spend confidently in retirement, so please be open to the best options for you *and* your heirs.

I KNOW WHAT I HAVE, NOW WHAT?

This is a daunting task for most individuals—how do I span that income gap, month after month and year after year? If your monthly income is $1,200 short, then focus your energy on what you're going to do to make sure you have $1,200 coming in from your retirement accounts.

I believe there are two main approaches to taking income in retirement:

First we have *the uncertain way:* to simply keep the money in investment accounts that have variable returns (they go up and down with the fluctuations of the stock market), take distributions, hold on like mad, and hope for the best.

In my opinion, relying on investments that fluctuate in value to pay most of your bills in retirement is the last thing you want to do. This approach results in uncertainty and carries an ever-looming possibility of running out of money.

When you were working, you probably employed a popular strategy called dollar-cost averaging, or DCA. The fancy definition of DCA is an investment strategy that aims to reduce the impact of volatility on purchases of financial assets through consistent periodic investments. While it doesn't assure a profit or guarantee against losses, it can to help reduce the effects of the market highs and lows by buying the same dollar amount in investments on a regular basis, regardless of the unit price.

DCA is an investment strategy that aims to reduce the impact of volatility on purchases of financial assets such as equities/stocks.

One common example is a 401(k). If you're investing in your 401(k) plan at work, then every two weeks, even before you get your paycheck, your 401(k) plan takes a portion from your check before you pay taxes or see any of that money.

The average American isn't saving much of their paycheck—most Americans don't have enough to cover a single $1,000 emergency.[23] You probably can't retire on that. As a woman, I usually suggest you want to shoot for closer to 14 percent or more of your paycheck going into your company's retirement plan, depending on your unique circumstances and time frame to retirement. You *pay yourself first*, not the IRS. That is the beauty of a company retirement plan (401(k), 403(b), TSP, SEP-IRA, etc.). You allocate money to your retirement savings BEFORE the IRS gets its hands on it (so you also pay less in current taxes). It is a great way to save automatically and efficiently. If you save 3, 4, or 6 percent from each paycheck, try to increase your contribution by 1 or 2 percent each year until you are at or above 14 percent. Most company plans have a feature that allows you to automatically increase your contribution by a certain percentage (say 1 percent) on a day of the year you determine (like the date when you receive a raise or bonus each year). Use it!

Every two weeks, the allocations are like clockwork. When the market is up, you buy shares at a higher price, but your previously purchased shares have also grown. When the market is down, your investment total may seem less impressive, but your money purchases more shares for a lower price than the prior ones. Those skinny shares will hopefully fatten when the market goes up again. Over time, it is a commonly used accumulation strategy designed to help grow your retirement account. Thus DCA (this consistent contribution) is viewed as a more effective investment strategy than if you would have stored up all those contributions and tried to time the market by putting it all in on one day and trying to ride the market roller coaster that way.

---

23 Maria Vultaggio. Statista. December 18, 2019. "Most Americans Lack Savings." https://www.statista.com/chart/20323/americans-lack-savings/

Well, sad to say, it works in reverse, too. Reverse dollar-cost averaging, or RDCA, is when you are making consistent withdrawals from your accounts, or selling off shares. When the market is up, you are selling fewer shares, but when the market is down, you have to sell off more shares to be able to meet your expenses (consider selling in March 2009, the lowest point in the market following the Great Recession), which also gives your account fewer assets to use to recover when the market bounces back.

So, is there another option when we want guaranteed income that doesn't exhibit RDCA?

Indeed, there is!

The certain way: you can add a level of certainty into your retirement income plan by implementing some form of guaranteed income by designating an amount of your retirement assets toward income creation. Various tools are specifically designed to generate income for retirees, similar to how a pension works.

When you work for a company that offers a pension, you usually have an option to take it in a lump sum or to receive it as an annuity (the term annuity means "fixed annual sum for the remainder of the annuitant's life"). Most people don't question the credibility of the Boeing or City of Seattle pension provider. But if you don't have a pension, then you should consider evaluating an alternative income option that also offers guaranteed income for life.

Even though pensions pay guaranteed annual income like annuities, we often see individuals conditioned to believe that all annuities are bad. Not so. You need to know the difference between those and which ones might best fit your needs.

VARIABLE ANNUITIES

Often when I speak about purchasing a guaranteed income annuity, a woman's face distorts, her body language shifts, and she says, "Yuck, I don't like annuities. I hear annuities are bad." It could be because some annuities are *not* suitable for retirees on a fixed income. Annuities have evolved over the years, so what you may know about annuities from decades ago is likely outdated. Let's cover the different types of annuities offered today.

Variable annuities (VA) are sold through brokerage channels with the positive features of lifetime income and the upside potential offered by the stock market (we all want that!). But what you need to understand is that they involve *inherent market risk* and market-related *fees*. Variable annuities involve market participation by investing in underlying mutual funds. Seems pretty glamorous—upside potential capable of gaining a lot in a raging bull market (super sexy), but they can deliver a significant hangover if the market goes through a major correction. The amount you gave to the insurance company (your principal amount) could lose value if the stock market tanks.

Additionally, there are three common types of variable annuity fees to be aware of:

1. Insurance fees, also known as mortality expense (M&E) fees, and administrative fees.

2. Investment management fees, similar to management fees on mutual funds.

3. Rider fees, for optional guarantees that there may be an increase in payments each year by a pre-set percentage to help keep up with inflation.

Additionally, if you withdraw more than the amount allowed in a given year, typically somewhere between 5 to 10 percent, you may incur a surrender charge.

Many clients who come in to see us are paying 3 to 4 percent in fees to own their variable annuities. That's a significant cost before you receive any benefit from the annuity. Being on a fixed income in retirement (remember, you don't have a paycheck any longer), you need to be mindful of the fees you are paying out of your retirement assets (more on this in Chapter Seven). With variable annuities' high fees and high market risk, variable annuities are not something I recommend for many retirees—retirement is a time to lower both fees and market risk.

IMMEDIATE ANNUITIES

Immediate annuities are another type of annuity. Immediate annuities provide the positive attribute of guaranteed income (which again, we love) that begins immediately, and they don't have stock market risk. But you give an amount of money to an insurance company, and they (not you) keep control over that money.

I believe that control and options in retirement are paramount.

Often, immediate annuities have a certain amount of time that they guarantee payments, like five years, and, if you die before the end of that time period, the insurance company sends your remaining payments to your named beneficiaries. But if you have an immediate annuity and you die in year six, in this example, the remaining principal balance will stay with the insurance company and not pay out to your beneficiaries. I don't like being out of control, and neither do you.

So, what are other possible positive options for retirement?

FIXED ANNUITIES

Fixed annuities are fixed insurance products. They don't have downside market risk. Like all annuities, an insurance company (not a bank) issues the contract and for a set time period, say three to five years (that is the interest rate guarantee period). They have a declared interest rate that is generally 1 percent or so higher than what you could get at a bank for a Certificate of Deposit (CD), but usually in line with current interest rates for the country.

It often can be a great benefit for my clients in their late eighties, or into their nineties, for example. But the declared interest rate usually is not much higher than the inflation rate. So it doesn't get me too excited to put a big portion of money there if we need to use it for current or future income and to outpace inflation.

FIXED INDEX ANNUITIES

Maybe you are one of the millions who aren't fortunate enough to have a robust pension, but you're looking for a financial vehicle that offers a similar stream of guaranteed income. I believe this income gap may be filled by fixed and guaranteed products (i.e. accounts that don't fluctuate with the market), which also allow you to control your principal. One such option we recommend, when prudent to do so, is a *fixed index annuity*, often with an optional *guaranteed lifetime withdrawal benefit* (GLWB) rider.

Fixed index annuities combine some of the upside potential for interest growth without being exposed to the downside risk of the market. They have the opportunity for steady, consistent income without losing control over your principal balance.

With a fixed index annuity, the costs of the product are built in, so you don't see added annual management fees or charges. The only fees you'll see deducted from your annuity value are for optional riders that you may select, such as the GLWB rider. These riders offer various features and guarantees, such as a potential increase in payments each year, or additional coverage for long-term care or other health care expenses.

HOW DO THEY WORK?

Sounds great, but what's the catch? Well, variable annuities and fixed index annuities are like any other financial product. There are terms, conditions, and limitations, and you need to decide if you can accept them, including a "surrender charge," a special fee that the insurance company might charge if you try to leave the contract early.

If you withdraw more than the amount allowed in a given year, typically somewhere between 5 and 10 percent, you may incur a surrender charge. There is a determined holding period (a period you are required to keep that contract with the insurance company) ranging from five to ten years for most annuities. If you pull out more money than the allotted amount, you may be charged a surrender penalty, in addition to ordinary income taxes payable. However, this fee is usually avoidable with proper planning.

This charge does not apply at death. Fixed index annuities become fully liquid at your death, so your heirs can usually receive the full remaining death benefit with no surrender penalties. We refer to them as having "limited liquidity," since they have a holding period of up to ten years. That's one reason I caution clients about "not overdoing it"; you want a good balance in your overall portfolio, not too much of anything—even a good thing.

If you add a proper dosage of one of these steady products into a well-diversified plan, it can do the job to generate income for you during retirement, similar to how a pension would have if you had been lucky enough to have one.

NO PERFECT TOOL

No matter what type of financial tool you use, you can typically only have two of these three attributes: growth potential, liquidity, and protection. Nothing that I know of offers all three.

Growth Potential and Liquidity: This would typically be your investment or brokerage account. You get the market's upside potential and at any time could cash that puppy in and get most or all of your money in a few days. But the downside is there isn't any safety component to it; there is no floor. If we hit another 2008-esque event, you could find yourself set back a couple of years or more and be emotionally (and financially) exhausted.

Liquidity and Protection: This would likely be your bank and money market money. It is readily available and FDIC-insured. This is a vital part of a healthy retirement plan. Confident spending typically comes from our accessible cash on hand. Most clients need a reasonable amount of liquid cash available at any given time, and the amount will vary by the client's situation. This is usually the account you draw out of for travel, gifting, fixing the water heater, or anything you desire to do now. The downside is you may receive close to "point nothing" in interest to have it just sitting there. Not much growth.

Protection and Growth Potential: This would be where fixed index annuities fall. You get the opportunity to earn interest tied to an external market index but, because it's guaranteed by the financial strength and claims-paying ability of the issuing company, your annuity value won't decrease due to a market decline. Up or flat, but never down. This can be a great component for a retiree, but one of the downsides is they lack the liquidity piece. You can cash it out at any time, but just like with a CD, you will pay the penalty for doing so in the early years of the contract. As I mentioned before, they have limited liquidity since there is a determined surrender charge or "holding" period of five, seven, or ten years for most.

When it comes to a significant other, one person can't meet every need for you, and neither can one single investment tool do all the work in your financial plan. But with great friends, family, church, clubs, etc., you can create a life that has all the important areas covered. You can live with great joy, peace, and health. A well-designed financial plan can help you do the same.

BUILD YOUR LIFE ON A SOLID FOUNDATION

After successfully imploding my life at twenty-four, I had a lot of time ahead of me to rebuild and recraft my life. If you are sixty-five, you may not have the luxury of a do-over. You don't want to get this "retirement thing" wrong. You need to take solid, well-founded advice from someone who specializes in retirement planning, because the investment rules you ran by in your twenties, thirties, and forties don't necessarily apply when you're in your sixties and beyond.

As you are interviewing a retirement planner or financial adviser, make sure they speak this language. If it is all about return on investments, stocks, bonds, and variable annuities, then run! If the conversation only centers around annuities and insurance, you are also limiting your success. Keep looking.

Remember the three foundational pillars we use at Becker Retirement Group:

Preservation of assets—guarding the money you worked so hard to accumulate and being sure it will be there for your whole life (not just for *most* of your life).

Income planning—using products and strategies that cover income gaps and planning to give you predictable paychecks to help you pay bills and *play*-checks to enjoy the opportunities life affords you.

Growth—once the areas of your needs and essentials (the concrete and the intangible) are covered, we use strategies aimed at growth to address longevity, inflation, future health care, and legacy needs.

RULE #1: DON'T LOSE MONEY. RULE #2: DON'T FORGET RULE #1.

Warren Buffet's famous rules of investing: Rule Number One: Don't Lose Money. Rule Number Two: Don't Forget Rule Number One. Buffet's wisdom becomes critical in retirement because losses are harder to recoup. Your lifespan shortens, and you have less capacity for risk (I address this more in Chapter Seven). It's not the time to bet the farm or to act in the same manner you did when you were trying to accumulate your retirement savings in your twenties, thirties, and forties.

It bears repeating. We need to make sure growth remains in its proper place.

The three-step approach we follow in our office helps our clients keep an appropriate blend of assets. We're trying to be sure that when inevitable market downturns occur, they don't lead to anxious moments, feelings of insecurity, and lack of control. Does this mean you go outside and bury everything in the back yard? Not at all. It means you adopt a well-conceived plan for how you're going to create an asset mix designed to weather any of the "what ifs" you may face.

WHAT IS A "GOOD" ASSET MIX?

Ideally, you'll have some portion of your portfolio that will be stable, another portion that has modest upside opportunity with good cash flow and liquidity, and another portion poised for growth that will help you combat inflation.

Finding the right balance across asset classes is key. From that point, you can begin selecting the individual tools within each asset category, all the while keeping the theme of preservation in mind. In retirement, slow and steady returns win the race.

Certainly, any solid plan needs to be monitored and adjusted periodically, so I suggest revisiting your plan at least annually. Above all, trust your gut. If you still feel like you have too much money at risk, speak to your adviser until your portfolio is rebalanced so you can live at peace without suffering gut checks each time the stock market ticker comes on the TV.

I'll end with this: Once I had the opportunity to dive with sting rays and black-tipped reef sharks in the tropics. It was pouring rain, and the water was choppy. The guides assured us our endeavor was perfectly safe, although the menacing weather told a different story. The moment I was just a couple feet below the surface, the storm raging above didn't affect me at all. I imagine farther out in the ocean, even the stronger squalls with tossing and roiling waves don't matter much to the marine life farther down. If your investments are appropriately placed, even with a serious market event, you can still weather the storm with relative ease and calm, and enjoy some fun sights along the way.

> *You can't go where you are going without leaving where you've been.*

MOST IMPORTANT TAKEAWAYS

1. Income overlaid with expenses is the crux of planning. What you have saved for retirement is second to that. Stop comparing to others and get the facts about your situation.

2. Mind the Gap—make sure you have a *written* income plan.

3. Inheritance is a bonus, so don't plan with it in mind, but a fun part-time job may be exactly what you need to pad your retirement picture perfectly.

4. Get all the facts about the Social Security benefits due to you (especially if married or divorced after a ten-plus year marriage); the same goes for your pension.

5. Shoot to save 14 percent (or more) in your company retirement plan or SEP-IRA and have an annual increase automated if that feature is available.

6. Not all annuities are the same. Understand the different types available and how they work to decide if one might be right for you.

7. Growth, protection, liquidity—you can only have two of three in any one type of financial tool.

8. As you enter your mid-fifties, you need to begin shifting your mindset from growth, growth, growth to preservation, income, *then* growth. Slow and steady.

NEXT STEPS

1. Find out how much money you will need once you stop working and have your financial adviser commit this income plan to paper. For marrieds, be sure this plan works (again, *on paper)* even when you account for the death of your spouse or partner at any age.

2. Ask your planner to show you how to optimize your Social Security and/or pension within the context of your plan, not in a micro-climate.

3. Right now, pull up your company retirement plan website, where you can see your account, and consider increasing it by 1 percent. See if there is a feature that will do this automatically for you annually. Use it!

4. If you are facing an income gap, ask your planner if an annuity could help solve it.

CHAPTER 7

MARKET RISK & FEES

Trials do not define, they refine.

RISK TOLERANCE VERSUS RISK CAPACITY

Seventy percent of women leave their financial advisers following the death of their spouse because the adviser didn't prepare them for the possibility of widowhood.[24]

Remember Lily from Chapter Four? She was the gal who suddenly lost her husband at fifty-nine. She hadn't worked for many years due to raising children and caring for her ailing mother for several years. She was part of the "sandwich generation," a woman who concurrently cares for children and a parent. That causes a drain on finances for anyone, but especially women.

When we finally dug into the specifics of her financial situation, I discovered Lily had $800,000 in retirement savings. There was no

---

24 Karen Demasters. "Widows' Voices: The Value of Financial Planning" as seen in *Financial Advisor Magazine. January 31, 2018. "How Advisors Can Tailor Their Services for Widows."* https://www.fa-mag.com/news/financial-life-after-widowhood-36922.html

pension, no life insurance proceeds, and the smaller of the two Social Security benefits stopped coming upon her husband's death. Not having a pension is common these days, and the loss of a spouse's Social Security is inevitable. But you can always have some form of life insurance. We will talk about that in Chapter Ten, but adequate insurance is one tool that can make a serious difference in keeping widows out of poverty.

Back to Lily. This $800,000 was everything to her and would need to last for possibly another forty years. Remember, she was fifty-nine. You may recall, her two highest priorities were never needing to return to work and never burdening her kids with her care. The thought of putting her kids through that hell made her skin crawl.

Financial security meant *everything* to her. Everything.

As we talked, I discovered her and her husband's assets had peaked at approximately $800,000 in 1999, followed by three years of "dot-bomb" losses (2000, 2001, 2002) that dropped their total by hundreds of thousands. Their accounts finally climbed back to the $800,000 watermark when I met her in June 2008. When I began a deep dive into what Lily had as investments with James, I realized she had a lot of concentrated stock in many beloved Northwest companies. I love supporting Northwest companies, but as my husband says, "too much of a good thing can make you sick or broke!" This led us into a serious conversation about her market risk.

Since the "dot-bomb" correction, Lily wasn't just widowed, but she was six years older than she had been. Half a decade can make a big difference in the time-horizon of a plan, and she discovered her accounts were much too volatile for her risk tolerance (emotional capacity to handle risk) and risk capacity (monetary capacity to handle risk).

There's a big difference between risk tolerance and risk capacity. Emotionally you might be able to tolerate risk and say, "Yeah, I can handle losing 25 percent." But, as a financial adviser, I might say, "Your retirement doesn't have the capacity for that. You do that and you could face the risk of running out of money before your time." You don't want that to happen. You must get your risk tolerance and risk capacity in line based on other factors in your life.

SHE CUT HOW MUCH OFF YOUR HAIR?

I was twenty-two before I let anyone other than my mom cut my hair. I have always had long hair, and I recall girls coming to school in junior high with short haircuts and shouting, "I went to the salon and she cut eight inches off my hair!" I had such a fear that I would go into a salon and some lady would chop my hair off (and get paid for it!) that I never went. When I was finally out of college and married, it seemed a bit weird to still let Mom cut my hair. I also realized I simply needed to communicate with my stylist about my preferences.

Cliché, but communication is key.

If I go into the salon and say, "I want a change. Something a bit edgy," the stylist's idea of "change" and "edgy" could be totally different than mine. Understanding risk is the same way. I will have prospective clients tell me, "I am a pretty moderate investor," but when I do a formal risk analysis, many of them test more conservative than they thought. If I took what they said, and applied my educated opinion of risk, I might just "chop off her hair," leaving her angry and disappointed at the next market correction.

That choice could alter your retirement. This is deeply vital to living the life you want and deserve.

"How do you feel about risk from one to ten?"

"Hmmmm . . ." you may answer, "Three."

But what does that really mean? Conservative? Is that 30 percent? Are you okay with 30 percent of your retirement money at risk? Do you think a 30 percent drop in your savings is fine? Applying a simple percentage in the assessment of risk is too vague. Nonetheless, planners across the country ask that question and then act on those assumptions, often putting you in a position that is too risky or (much rarer but still detrimental) too conservative. You need to have a much clearer determination of risk.

How much of your retirement assets (in dollars and cents) are you willing to put on the craps table that is the stock market? How much are you potentially willing to lose over the next six months? Answer that question, and we start to have some clear direction toward developing a retirement plan.

CERTIFICATES OF DEPOSIT TO ELON MUSK

We have an exceptional and simple tool that helps identify risk. The program has risk numbers ranging from one, which is guaranteed, to ninety-nine, most aggressive. Guaranteed would entail cash, CDs, fixed annuities, and fixed index annuities. None has much risk of market loss—CDs and bank accounts are insured by the banks and the Federal Deposit Insurance Corporation (FDIC), and annuities are guaranteed by the financial strength of their issuing company. Then you run up the risk ladder through bonds, REITs, variable annuities, and stocks to hang out with your buddy, Elon Musk, and his company, Tesla, at a risk number of ninety-nine, in my book.

Our software works by dissecting your portfolio, individually assessing the risks and fees you take with each annuity, REIT, CD, stock, ETF, bond, mutual fund, etc. Based on the way these products all work together, the computer assigns your household an overall risk score.

This risk score tells you what portion of your assets could potentially drop or go up in the next six months, and by how much. Often, those calculations will make a woman begin to sweat or feel sick to her stomach, as if it is actually happening. It's a visceral reaction and, candidly, it should be. This is all the money you have to sustain your lifestyle for the rest of your life. Any pain you feel should inspire you to act.

This scoring is critical in helping us avoid micro-climate plans. I don't want to make suggestions regarding your IRA or brokerage account that might duplicate investments you already have in a 401(k) at work. It could be shortsighted to pursue a hefty annuity contract if you'll be drawing a sizeable pension from work or on a spouse's record. You need to be sure that you're considering all your holdings, even if the adviser you're working with can't or doesn't personally manage it.

HOW MUCH ARE YOU REALLY WILLING TO LOSE?

Now we need to do the second part. We take your total retirement asset value (not your net worth or home value, but the value of all your accounts—banking, brokerage, investment, annuity, etc.) and use that to determine the risk questions we are going to walk through. So, the amount of money you have for retirement, a dollar figure, is going to help us identify the amount of money you are willing to potentially lose in the next six months if a major market correction occurred. Or, let me put it this way: You open your brokerage statement and you see that you have lost "X" amount of money in the last six months. We don't just put it in terms of percentages; we'll talk about it in terms of dollars and cents, a subtle shift that can radically change the way people think and talk about their risk tolerance.

I follow up with, "With the risk number you just tested out at, it says you are okay with possibly losing X amount of your money in six months. Are you okay with that?"

Your answer may be, "Yeah, I'm okay with that. I understand risk and reward." Or you may look disgusted and say, "Absolutely not! I'm not willing to lose that much!" If that is the case, you need to reduce the risk of your holdings to be in line with what you're *emotionally* comfortable with. That's risk tolerance.

So, let's see how this exercise looked for Lily.

LOOKING CALIFORNIA, FEELING MINNESOTA

Growing up in Seattle and going to college during the early nineties grunge era, I was a huge fan of the band Soundgarden. One famous song, early in the band's career, was called "Outshined." There is a line I love that the late Chris Cornell wrote as he felt a bit frumpy, but caught a glance of himself in the mirror wearing board shorts and a T-shirt: "looking California, feeling Minnesota." Those weren't my words, so if you are from Minnesota, please don't shoot the messenger.

That echoes a sense of living aggressively but feeling conservative. I think that when comparing those two states, that line could very much have applied to Lily's situation regarding risk; *looking aggressive, feeling conservative* seemed to be an apt description. Lily's household risk score was seventy-four, but her risk tolerance was thirty-one, a massive discrepancy!

I said, "Okay, Lily, I believe we need to do some rebalancing of your current holdings to get your entire investment household in line with your current risk number (tolerance) of thirty-one. It could be a major blow to your retirement portfolio if you went through a major market correction when you are living a seventy-four (looking aggressive) but desiring a thirty-one (feeling conservative)."

She agreed that a significant change was in order. So, I began to show her ways we could correct her incongruity.

Looking aggressive but feeling conservative. Grounds for emotional and financial destruction.

REBALANCING

So many women find themselves in Lily's position of risk discrepancy at her age. You have worked with blinders on, contributing to your company plan, and the Great Recession seemed to be in the rearview mirror for a time. I implore you to discuss with your adviser your current risk posture. I have sat with hundreds of women who have just left their assets alone for decades. The equity positions (growth stocks) did very well, whereas bonds (less risky income producers) have performed poorly during a period of low interest rates.

This causes an out-of-balance portfolio that begins to shift out of the investment posture you were comfortable with a few years ago. Make sure you are revisiting this every couple of years. We do a new risk test every year for our clients to make sure their assets are still in line with what they can emotionally tolerate.

Remember our three foundational pillars as a company: preservation of assets, income planning, and *then* growth. Those components need to stay in the proper order when you are in retirement, and they can only do that when you have a clear plan based on sound research and experience, not just what worked in the past. Financial catastrophes, like those we are now seeing with the effects of the coronavirus pandemic, can be prepared for. It is possible to weather even another recession (or maybe worse) if preservation is always first and foremost in the plan.

Back to Lily.

Once we had addressed her risk posture, we began to evaluate the "what-ifs" of longevity, nursing home care, or a major market correction. We hope to virtually eliminate any possibility of a "redline" (running out of money before age one hundred), or at least push it out as far as we can with planning. For her, the changes we suggested were intended to potentially eliminate her risk of ever running out of money.

She was ready to handle it.

We began crafting a *Best Life Retirement Plan* for Lily. She marveled at the simplicity of the outline and how she could understand it quite easily. We started the initial process of bringing her assets over to our custodian and under our care. She signed all the initial paperwork to move her accounts, though we weren't at the place yet where we were liquidating or buying anything. We spent the rest of the visit talking about scripture verses and quotes she was thinking about putting on a memorial bench for her husband at a park near their home.

She left our office with hugs. Victory!

Until…

Four days later, she called and was apologetic.

"You know, Arwen, thank you so much for the effort. I really appreciate all your help, but I'm going to cancel the plan. I talked to my son, and he said, 'You know, Mom, it sounds a little conservative to me. Honestly, I'm not really that familiar with some of the investment tools that you said they're using. I really think that you should talk to your broker first (the one her and her husband had worked with those years before) and get his opinion.'"

Sheepishly, she took his advice.

YOUR HUSBAND TRUSTED ME; I HOPE YOU WOULD, TOO

Lily called the broker and did her best to explain what I had proposed for her, since she didn't have her completed *Best Life Retirement Plan* in hand—it wasn't finalized yet. Imagine, a woman detached from her finances over the years, trying to explain to a seasoned financial veteran what we had suggested over three visits. It's like me explaining to a new occupational therapist how the brain exercises recently assigned to my son, who has ADHD and graphomotor issues, are going to help solve his neurological problems.

Impossible.

We were only in the beginning phases of crafting her retirement plan, but she did her best to explain to her longtime adviser what it was I had proposed. He created doubts for Lily about this new path, and said, "You know what, Lily, our plan (her old plan) is a great plan and we're going to stay the course and, honestly, your husband trusted me all these years, I would really hope that you trust me on this one."

So, she stayed. Reluctantly, it seemed, based on how she relayed this latest development to us.

In my opinion, she questioned herself and betrayed her intuition.

Later on, when the market was in recession, I couldn't help but think of Lily and wonder how she was doing.

To this day, I wonder if her original plan worked, if she had to go back to work or, as she is now seventy, whether she needs some type of care and must rely on her children. When finances become depleted, and financial strain ensues, the property taxes must still get paid, prescriptions must still be taken, and often the fun stuff must be put aside or forgotten entirely.

When you have a clear plan based on sound research and experience, not just what feels good or what worked in the past, you can avoid catastrophes like this.

CAREFULLY WEIGH WELL-MEANING ADVICE — TRUST WOMEN'S INTUITION

You may be a woman who doesn't deeply understand all the ins and outs I am speaking about, but you need to trust your intuition when things just don't feel right. Many ladies get derailed, going against their gut even when they can't exactly explain why they feel that way. If you have an adviser, family member, or friend who is pressuring you to do something that doesn't feel right, remember this is your money and your future. Many women have been hurt when they questioned their gut and betrayed their intuition.

You *can* make great decisions. Just make sure you feel a peace and ease with the adviser you are dialoguing with. You are very able!

IT'S TIME IN THE MARKET, NOT TIMING THE MARKET

"Arwen, call us first thing tomorrow, we want to liquidate everything to cash!"

The time stamp on that voicemail was 11:43 p.m. on Donald Trump's election night. I called those clients back the next day and did my best to deter them from making such a rash, emotionally based decision, but they wouldn't budge. I called the trading desk and instructed them to liquidate the $320,000 the couple had invested in the stock market to cash.

That began one of the best first hundred days in the market of a presidential term.[25]

The problem with timing the market is you must be right twice. You need to be right as to when to get out, and you need to be right as to when you should get back in. The problem is, no one ever knows when the market is going to go up or down. They can speculate, but the words *speculate* and *retirement* do not belong in the same sentence.

You're smart, and you know that.

Retirement planning isn't about short bursts in and out of the market. You need a long-term strategy that allocates some money to risk and growth opportunity, and that has the time to recover when the market gyrates or corrects. Markets usually recover, at least to a certain extent. But the challenge is, we don't know how long that may take, and the correction may come at the worst time for you: at the beginning of your retirement journey.

The couple who called on election night missed some of the best growth during those early Trump years because they made an emotional decision, not one based on long-term planning.

Do not work with anyone who tells you they know how to time the market. The time for rational, long-term planning begins now, not "when the market comes back."

---

25   Mark DeCambre. MarketWatch. April 30, 2017. "How Trump's Stock Market Ranks During His First 100 Days in Office." https://www.marketwatch.com/story/how-trumps-stock-market-ranks-on-his-100th-day-in-office-2017-04-29

MORE OPTIONS IN AN IRA — IN-SERVICE DISTRIBUTION

Multiple times through the last ten years, I actively withdrew money out of my mom's 401(k) and deposited those funds into an actively managed IRA. That action is called an *in-service distribution*. It's where you're still employed with your company and actively contributing to your company's retirement plan, but you can withdraw the money saved in your company plan, roll it into an IRA (not a bank account, so you don't cause a taxable event), and then you have additional investment options available to you, not just the limited few options in your company's retirement plan. You typically shouldn't do an in-service distribution before turning fifty-nine-and-one-half, however, or you will receive a 10 percent penalty from the IRS (Uh, no thank you).

My mom wanted these rollovers to lessen her investment in Costco stock, which was very aggressive (as of today, a risk number of seventy-two). She wanted to start protecting those assets, to make sure they would be there for her after forty years of hard work. Many women I speak with are, like my mom, conservative investors. They cite financial security as their most important value. If that is you, it is often wise to turn to tools with some growth potential and little to no downside risk.

LESS RISK THE OLDER WE GET

Words I never hear as ladies embark on retirement: "I want things to be riskier and more complicated." Oh, please. The older you get, the more risk-averse you become, and the more you want things simple and organized. Risk reduction and management are the most common areas I work on with new clients. It is not at all uncommon for a potential client to come in, newly retired or just about ready to retire, and have 75 to 95 percent of their assets invested in the stock market. Historically, the market delivers the best growth potential, pound for pound, and is where most of us grow, accumulate, and save money for retirement. But nearing retirement, the percentages need to trend lower.

Here is a very simple rule of thumb to determine if you need to think about shifting the proportion of assets you have at risk.

RULE OF 100

The Rule of 100 is a general principle that says, if you subtract your age from 100, the result is the percentage of your assets that you can invest at risk. So, if you are sixty years old, you subtract your age from 100, and what you have remaining, forty, is the responsible percentage to keep at risk. If you are married, you average your ages and then do the same thing. If you have north of 70 percent of your retirement assets at risk, you should strongly think about moving assets from a place of high risk to low risk or no risk.

As I said, it's just a general principle—factors such as the amount of assets you have, your legacy goals, your health care plans, your planned retirement date, and others will affect the picture.

Our team at Becker Retirement Group performs a much more thorough analysis of your risk tolerance and capacity, but at least this very simple "rule" can give you a little direction as you get closer to retirement. If you work with an adviser whose allocation recommendations are far off of the quick marginal calculation of the Rule of 100, ask why and be sure they have a very satisfactory answer.

LOTS OF EGGS, LOTS OF BASKETS

Now that you have a good indication of how much money to retain in a position of accelerated growth potential and risk, we want to make sure those assets are more broadly *diversified*. When you are looking at ways to keep growth potential in your retirement plan, you want broad diversification; a lot of eggs in a lot of baskets.

Some of our professionally managed portfolios have up to 6,000 stocks and 5,000 bonds represented in them, spanning sixty countries and eighteen asset classes. That's broad diversification. You want to cover a great deal of financial landscape, so if one area is burning to the ground, another area might just be rising from the ashes. But recall, you told me you didn't want it more complicated, so that account with all that broad diversification might have only fifteen to twenty holdings (line items on your statement).

It's broad diversification, simplified.

Women don't want to get sixty-two-page statements. Simplified, yet diversified, is the way to go to lessen your potential harm by a market correction.

SORRY, DEAR, YOU'RE PAYING $18,000 IN FEES, NOT $3,600

"How much do you pay your financial adviser to manage this account?" That's a common question I will ask a prospective client. Many women can answer that question. They'll say something like 1 percent or 1.5 percent. Other times, they aren't entirely sure.

I had this gal come in who had $1.5 million managed by an adviser, so I asked, "Well, how much do you pay the adviser to manage that?"

She hesitated, then said, "Well, I think about $300 a month."

I just looked at her, a bit puzzled, and said, "I am sorry, my dear, but I don't think that any adviser would manage that amount of money for only $300 a month. Could I see a statement?"

She got online and pulled off the statement. I looked through it and I said, "Well, I've got to tell you, we're about halfway through the year, and you've already paid about $9,000 in fees."

She was paying about six times more than she thought.

And those were the fees she *could* see on her statement.

FEES YOU CAN'T SEE

The truth is advisory fees are not bad if you're receiving value for them, but often it's the internal fees individuals have zero clue about. Internal fees (internal expense ratios) are the administrative costs associated with a mutual fund, REIT, or ETF. For example, if you own a mutual fund, which is a big basket of holdings (i.e., stocks, bonds, etc.), there's a team of people "inside" that fund making decisions on your behalf. A little less here, little more there, kick that stock out, bring in this bond. When that happens, there are administrative costs paid to the team that manages it.

Unless you love to jump on the internet and research every mutual fund or ETF you own, most women are completely in the dark as to the amount they pay for internal expenses. You won't ever see these fees on your statements; instead, you need to read a fund's complex and lengthy prospectus to find this information. When we work through our risk software, I can show you immediately how much you pay internally for your entire household (every holding), and that is before the adviser managing it gets their cut in advisory fees.

I regularly see prospective clients with holdings that cost, internally, north of 2 percent. Sometimes I've seen funds with costs at almost 4 percent! Add a 4 percent expense ratio to a 1.5 percent advisory fee, and you need to gross 5.5 percent just to break even. This is expensive and, in most cases, completely unnecessary.

To be clear, unless you are a broker who can spend time privately negotiating trade deals for each stock with a company, the services that each layer of management provides on your behalf are completely necessary. You can't get something for nothing. But it's also true that you should get what you pay for. If one company charges you 3 percent, they better darn well be able to explain why they are so much better than the one down the street charging 1 percent. In my experience, most can't.

When we're working on our highly diversified portfolios, we try to keep the internal fees below 0.6 percent. Since you are on a fixed income once you retire, anything that robs your growth and sends money somewhere other than your pocket is affecting your Return on Retirement (ROR).

Know your numbers. It matters. You matter.

> *Belief without effort is a total waste of time. You must back up your faith with action.*

MOST IMPORTANT TAKEAWAYS

1. 70 percent of women leave their financial advisers following the death of their spouse.

2. *Risk tolerance* is your emotional ability to handle risk, and *risk capacity* is how much your money can handle.

3. Trust your gut intuition, even if you don't understand why.

4. It is time *in* the market, not timing the market. You need to be right twice. Those aren't good odds in your favor.

5. Most companies allow an *in-service distribution* at fifty-nine-and-one-half without penalty, and it can be a great idea with more investment choices available than you will have inside your company's plan.

6. The Rule of 100 is a simple way to estimate the reasonable risk for your current age.

7. Commonly misunderstood fees include the expenses you can't see on your statement for the investments you own.

8. Broad diversification and simplicity are beautiful words in retirement.

9. A great adviser is worth their advisory fee, and then some.

NEXT STEPS

1. If you aren't sure of the relationship with your adviser and you are married, either reach out to have a meeting (maybe one-on-one) to make sure you build that communication, or have the tough conversation with your spouse about looking for an adviser that connects well with *both* of you. Come on, girl, you can handle it!

2. At your next meeting (call and set one up with them, if necessary), have your adviser identify your true risk tolerance in dollars and cents as it relates to your retirement assets. If your adviser doesn't test for this, I suggest you look for someone who does.

3. Rebalance your portfolio immediately (if you haven't in the past eighteen months) if it's no longer in line with your desired risk tolerance. Make sure you discuss your risk tolerance with your adviser and that they can show you how your current holdings are *clearly* in line with how you *now* feel about risk, not how you felt eighteen months ago. You may need to retest your tolerance.

4. If you are approaching or past fifty-nine-and-one-half, ask your adviser what they would recommend for you regarding an in-service distribution of your company plan.

5. Ask your adviser to remind you what their advisory/management fees are to manage your assets and to do a complete fee analysis for your entire household of investments. If they can't, find an adviser who can.

CHAPTER 8

TAXES & REQUIRED MINIMUM DISTRIBUTIONS

> *Before the battle with your hands*
> *comes the battle in your mind.*

50% OFF: GREAT FOR A NORDSTROM SALE, NOT IN IRS PENALTIES

"Didn't your adviser tell you to take your RMDs?" By the look on their faces, you could see they had no idea what he was talking about. In 2010, we brought on a full-service tax practice that afforded us the ability to have certified public accountants prepare individual and business returns for our clients and many folks in our community. This couple was discussing their 1040 with Randy before they took it home, but were not retirement planning clients.

Randy continued as he poured over the couple's tax return from the previous year. "I should have seen some income on this line right here for your IRAs. Now that you're both seventy-two, each of you should have taken your RMD from your IRAs last year." As Randy looked at the couple's year-end statements, he found that, according to the IRS's life expectancy table, they should have withdrawn $30,000 from their IRAs for their Required Minimum Distribution (RMD).

They hadn't needed it for their expenses, so they hadn't thought to make the withdrawal. Failure to do so had cost them a hefty penalty—one of the largest penalties in the tax code: The IRS takes a 50 percent tax of missed RMDs. For this couple, $15,000 of their missed RMD went straight to Uncle Sam.

You will spend a great deal of your life accumulating much of your wealth in qualified plans—401(k)s, 403(b)s, 401 (a)s, TSPs, etc.—or Individual Retirement Accounts—IRAs, SIMPLE-IRAs, SEP-IRAs, etc. These are wonderful vehicles for saving money and accumulating wealth. You are taking a portion of your paycheck, a.k.a. *paying yourself first* (even before the sneaky IRS gets its hands in it). Then, the IRS will take its cut of what's left of your paycheck, and you get to take home what's left. Saving this way, you pay less in taxes along the journey because the IRS hasn't taken its cut of those retirement funds yet.

Operative word: *yet*.

HAPPY BIRTHDAY FROM THE IRS

It's early in January, and you blow out the candles on your birthday cake, the big 7-0! You are in the golden years of your life. You are toasting your good health and all your loved ones. Friends are in attendance cheering you on, and the adorable grandkids who love to spend time with Nana (or Nona, Mammaw, Gigi, or Grandma) are delightfully giggling in the backyard and rolling around in the newly cut grass. Ushering in seventy has been a bittersweet moment for you. Wisdom abounds, but many years are now behind you. Years of life have gone by. Occasionally, memories of regrets pass through your mind, so you are determined to make the remaining moments count.

This new decade is packed full of book clubs, gardening, painting with watercolors, volunteering, or going on two-week cruises to the Mediterranean or the Caribbean. Life is good, and the essential things have their proper place. The days blaze into weeks, and you're pleading with time to slow down while it blows by at hyper speed.

Seventy-two has now come and gone, and you file your tax return on time before the April 15th deadline. Well done!

Wait a second. You didn't stop to consider your seventy-second birthday? How can that be? You didn't think about your seventy-second birthday?

You were busy enjoying that wonderfully long cruise with your sister, and you failed to recognize the implications of your seventy-second birthday. Not the IRS, however. It remembered.

You have delayed paying taxes on your qualified plans your whole life and now the IRS wants its cut of your money and will demand it at the rate it feels is appropriate; hence the term *required minimum distribution*. You could pay taxes when the money goes in (the seed). That's what happens when you contribute to a Roth IRA—you pay taxes upfront and, if you abide by the terms of the plan, never have to worry about the IRS coming for those monies again. However, you chose to take the current tax break allowed with a pre-tax contribution while working. The IRS will want its cut of the harvest. From that point forward, the IRS collects an RMD and will expect that payment every year for the rest of your life at the rate it determines appropriate.

Prior to the Secure Act at the end of 2019, the IRS required you to start taking your RMDs at age seventy-and-one-half, but that was somewhat more confusing than the now-straightforward seventy-two rule.

For the couple at the beginning of this chapter, their previous adviser's oversight cost them $15,000. That would have paid for a three-week cruise for many of our more frugal couples. What a rip-off, one of the consequences of neglectful planning.

LET'S AVOID A 50% MISTAKE

As planners who focus specifically on retirement, this RMD tax bomb looming in the distance is a constant focus for us. Even if you are fifty-five when we sit down for the first time, we are going to be looking at your future tax bill once you hit seventy-two. You can do considerable planning seven to fifteen years away from that RMD time period, but once you hit it, there is little left but to take it and pay the tax. I understand, this is very much a first-world problem, but you don't want to find yourself in the same boat as many of our older clients who pay more in taxes at age seventy-five than they ever did while they were working. This is a big part of the reason that we have a CPA on staff to help avoid these major, unexpected tax bombs *and* to make sure you don't mess up your RMDs.

We work with people, not just money, and if you are with an adviser who has not spoken to you about your future tax bill *and* provided ideas and direction for how to reduce that, I would think long and hard if they are the best place for you over the long term.

On occasion, a woman might struggle to consider changing advisers. We hear, "Well, I will have to go back to my (current) adviser and ask them why we haven't talked about this and what to do about my RMD." My question back to her at that moment is always, "I understand what you mean, but doesn't it concern you that *you* have to bring up that topic with your adviser? Isn't that their job, as the expert, to bring to your attention what you need to do? It would make me wonder what other things they might be missing or failing to mention."

You may get a do-over as a kindergartner, but as a retiree, you get only one chance to do this right. You deserve a proactive approach to your retirement. You need to have a great coach who specializes in retirement and will arm you with all the planning, tools, and understanding you need to get this right the first time.

HOW IS IT CALCULATED?

The IRS has a tax table based on life expectancy that dictates you withdraw a certain percentage of your qualified plan total. In plain language, that means each year as you age, the IRS will require you to withdraw X amount (starting with 3.65 percent when you're seventy, and increasing each year to 52.63 percent for anyone 115 or older) from the combined total of your IRAs or similar plans.

STUFFED AND CONTENT OR OVERSTUFFED AND MISERABLE

On Mother's Day morning, you forced yourself to stay on the treadmill a bit longer, choked down a tiny, bland, protein shake for breakfast, and, by design, felt starved by noon. Church is over and you are now on your way in your oversized, light pink sweater and stretchy slacks (with your Spanx hiding beneath) to the town's best brunch buffet for Mother's Day. Your kids and grandkids are treating you, and the spread is amazing. Prime rib, giant prawns, waffles with bananas, eggs benedict, mini crème brûlées, and a mimosa bar; and that's just a small sampling of the yummy delights. Mmmmmm! You knew this brunch was coming, and you did all you could to prepare for the large, wonderful meal that lay ahead.

You were creating a hunger gap and using it.

YOUR TAX GAP

You are now sixty-three, have enjoyed many years working as a schoolteacher, but your pension doesn't turn on till sixty-five, and you have determined you'd like to delay your Social Security till seventy. Your RMD lies ahead, like your Mother's Day brunch, but at this moment in time, there is a gap—a wonderful, beneficial gap.

I love these gaps, and so should you.

A gap such as this is an ideal time to consider evacuating some of the money in your IRA while you have little to no income coming in. This means you are in a lower tax bracket, currently, so if you pull the income you need to bridge the income gap between your pension and Social Security, you will pay a lower rate in taxes to use the IRA monies you have *and* you will have a smaller tax bomb ahead of you when RMDs begin.

This is just good planning.

Alternatively, you could consume a pumpkin scone and Grande mocha at Starbucks just before church. At that point, 763 calories firmly planted in your stomach, you will still feel obligated to eat the afternoon brunch. "I never get these kinds of foods, and the kids went to all this trouble to bring me. It's expensive. I better eat a bit more." We have all made that mistake before.

We're left overstuffed and miserable.

This is a very common occurrence for retirees who pay more in taxes at seventy-five than when they were working. They neglected proper planning while in their fifties and sixties. Now, they are collecting a pension, Social Security, and RMDs. When you are forced to pull out—and pay taxes on—income you don't need, it is frustrating. Maddening, in fact.

For some clients, this income gap also creates a great time to consider Roth conversions. Roth IRAs are a good opportunity for many because you pay taxes on the money going in (the seed), but the harvest accumulates and comes out tax-*free*! It can be tough to build up a Roth while you are in the life-stage of saving and accumulating your wealth, which is why most of us have regular 401(k)s or IRAs. But, by gradually paying taxes on and converting these regular accounts to Roth accounts, which have no RMDs, are not taxed, and even pass to beneficiaries tax-free, you can avoid RMDs.

So, if you were to convert Traditional IRA funds to a Roth IRA, you would pay taxes on all the funds you convert in a given year. Provided the Roth IRA has been open for at least five years, you can take any withdrawals after fifty-nine-and-a-half as tax-free money.

Paying less in taxes now *and* in the future is obviously the ideal situation, but you may need help knowing how to execute Roth IRA conversions and what path is right for you. We have our CPA run scenarios for our clients to determine how we can help them maximize the income gap during their retirement. Make sure you understand this concept when you are speaking with your retirement planner. Ask them what type of tax planning they do to help reduce your future tax bill. Your seventy-five-year-old self will thank you. Also, it's fun to stick your seventy-two-year-old tongue out at the IRS and say, "Pbssst! Neener, neener, neener! I beat you!"

THAT WILL BE $90,000 IN TAX — BRING YOUR CHECKBOOK

Dottie and Ray had been clients of ours for more than ten years. They had been married for forty-five years and lived in their home for thirty-two years. When Ray began to struggle at finding his words and recalling elementary information, Dottie recognized something wasn't right. It was just a matter of eighteen months from the onset of dementia to when she found herself afraid of leaving her husband alone.

The terrible realization hit hard; he needed to move into a long-term care facility.

Dottie went through the agonizing effort to move her best friend into a facility near her home.

Their home was more than she wanted to maintain alone, and it was a harsh reminder of her husband's absence. She decided it was time to sell the memories, both great and not-so-great. The pain of his absence, along with the added pressure of living alone in a big house, was greater than the joy of the memories they had enjoyed within those walls.

Bittersweet, but she handled it.

The area that Dottie and Ray lived in was experiencing massive growth. In the 1980s, they had purchased their home for $265,000. When Dottie's real estate agent placed it on the market, it was snatched up nearly overnight for $1.4 million. WOW! Even factoring in $100,000 of improvements over the years, they made about a million dollars from the sale. Of course, some of that was inflation value, right? Well, while the IRS cut them some slack—$250,000 each, to be exact. The result was that Dottie still got a notice that she would need to cut the IRS a check for $90,000.

After processing the sticker shock, Dottie decided to consult the CPA that rents part of our office to see if she could reduce that bill.

The CPA asked for her tax returns from the past five years and discovered a "gift" from the past. Many years ago, Ray had sold some stocks at a loss, creating a large capital loss that became a "future gift" to his wife, though at the time I'm sure Ray had been very disappointed.

The day that Dottie arrived at the office to finalize her planning and find out the outcome of the CPA's findings, she had her checkbook and was reluctantly ready to write a $90,000 check to the IRS. The CPA, however, had some good news. Thanks to the capital loss from several years before, she would only have to pay $40,000.

Fifty thousand dollars saved!

The net effect of tax efficiency is just unreal.

When you are on a fixed income in retirement (no longer getting a paycheck), any amount of money you can save in taxes just means there is more money that will remain in your retirement for your future.

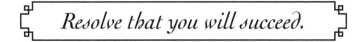

Resolve that you will succeed.

MOST IMPORTANT TAKEAWAYS

1. Required Minimum Distributions (RMDs) start the *year following* the year you turn seventy-two.

2. Unpaid RMDs carry a 50 percent penalty. But if you did miss it the first time, ask your planner or CPA to assist you in writing the IRS. They will often waive the penalty the first time but won't be so generous the next.

3. Income gaps can be opportunities to begin reducing your future RMD tax bill, but you need to be thinking about this in your late fifties and early sixties.

NEXT STEPS

1. Ask your adviser what the plan is for RMD tax savings and if the adviser's firm partners with a CPA. If that firm can't give you sound direction on RMDs, you may have outgrown your adviser and should consider partnering with someone who specializes in retirement planning.

2. Consider setting up an *automated* RMD. This way, you always know it pays on time, the IRS is satisfied, and you might have a time of year where an influx of money would be helpful for you.

CHAPTER 9

LONGEVITY & HEALTH CARE

Current discipline or future regret.
The choice is yours.

PAP SMEARS MAY SAVE MY SONS' LIVES

There's one commonality with most college students—they're usually broke. I was no exception. After giving up my full-ride scholarships to follow my boyfriend to the University of Washington, I didn't have time to get a job because Division I volleyball required a five-hour commitment each day. Our conditioning workouts lasted from 5:30 to 7 a.m. We practiced from 2:30 to 5:30 p.m. Between those sessions, we attended class. From 6 to 8 p.m., we participated in a mandatory study hall. Doesn't that sound like a party?

When I was approached as a freshman to join a cancer study that paid $10 every quarter and included free checkups, I jumped at the chance and didn't ask many questions.

I was one of 500 freshmen women who agreed to participate in this study. UW hoped to determine the precursor for cervical cancer, a noble aim I barely registered, as I just wanted the cash.

Once I committed to the study, I went to my first appointment and learned the protocol. For the next four years, I agreed to participate in four visits each year and was paid $10 for each visit. Each required an hour for me to go to the hospital, divulge my private information to a gynecologist, and have two blood draws, a pelvic exam, and SIX pap smears! *What did I get myself into?* It quickly became apparent that this four-year commitment was not worth the lousy compensation.

But I'm not a quitter.

Two years and eight appointments in, the research yielded such significant results that UW received another large grant to continue the study and add another 500 girls. Program administrators asked the first group to remain in the study for a few additional years.

In the end, I participated for ten years! My commitment to engage in sixteen appointments grew to twenty-eight. By the time the ten years had passed, eighty-seven women from the first group remained.

Remarkable.

But the most incredible part of that experience for me came twenty-five years after I had first signed up.

I took my middle son, Ashton, in for his twelve-year-old check-up. The doctor checked over his vaccination records and then asked if I wanted him to receive the HPV vaccine. The HPV vaccine helps protect against certain types of viruses that can lead to cancer, particularly cervical cancer. The vaccine was developed with research from a study the University of Washington began twenty-five years before, with 500 broke freshman girls, including me.

Committing to that study in 1993 was not an act of love, but desperation. I needed the money. After my first visit, though, I had two choices—be a woman of commitment or quit because it was hard, inconvenient, and very uncomfortable. All three of my boys, and their future wives, will benefit because eighty-seven women, including me, didn't quit.

I know you are just like me. You don't quit when things get tough.

LONGEVITY MIGHT BE THE BIGGEST RISK YOU FACE — COMMIT TO YOUR DAILY HEALTH

In the area of health and health care, there is a lot to be said about commitment. I am proud to have been a part of such a ground-breaking study that has affected millions of families during my lifetime. Now, longevity has the potential to be the biggest risk you face, possibly even more than market risk, taxes, or inflation. In the past 120 years, a woman's life expectancy has increased from forty-nine to eighty-one.[26]

Retirement, as we know it, didn't exist 120 years ago. If you were alive, you worked.

MEDICARE COST-SHIFTING

Longevity runs in Randy's family. His great aunt Louise lived till ninety-one. Her brother, great uncle Dan, lived till ninety-six, and their oldest sister, Randy's grandmother, Agnes, lived till a few months shy of her 101st birthday! Those were all on his mom's side. His dad's mother, Olive, also lived till ninety-seven…wow!

Having started in the retirement planning business in the late eighties, Randy was intimately aware and often involved in the discussions regarding the health care of those wonderful people, since neither Dan nor Louise had children of their own. What he saw

---

26 Social Security Administration. Actuarial Study No. 120. "Life Tables for the United States Social Security Area 1900-2100." https://www.ssa.gov/oact/NOTES/as120/images/LD_fig2a.html

regarding what Medicare covered in the early nineties versus what it covered when Grandma Agnes passed in 2013 was very different.

He saw firsthand that Medicare shielded the family from much of the dramatic burden of Olive's care in the nineties, when she battled through Alzheimer's for nearly seven years. Certainly, the family wished it would have covered more, since her long-term care policy eventually ran dry, but Medicare did pick up a large portion of that financial drain.

As Louise, Dan, and Agnes continued to age, as well as Randy's father, John, Randy became increasingly aware that Medicare was not covering many of the costs associated with their care, as it had with Olive decades before. Medicare had largely shifted the burden for their care back to them personally.

That's frightening.

The consequences of this are very real in terms of dollars and cents: One estimate says a couple, age sixty-five, average health, can expect to spend $285,000 on expenses related to health care in retirement.[27]

INVESTMENTS ARE NOT A "LIFE" PLAN

We won't avoid this necessary discussion. When you begin to look toward retirement, you don't need just a mix of stocks, bonds, variable annuities, and mutual funds—you need a soundly constructed, holistic plan. How will your plan pay for future health care should you need it for yourself or your spouse? How will your retirement assets cover future health care, especially if you don't have any children that could or would bear that burden if the money ran out?

Everyone deserves to be educated if they seek help. I became a financial adviser determined to help women prepare a *life* plan. With my fire sufficiently ignited to assist the underserved half of my community—women—I know it is never too late to become who

---

27 Fidelity Viewpoints. April 1, 2019. "How to Plan for Rising Health Care Costs." https://www.fidelity.com/viewpoints/personal-finance/plan-for-rising-health-care-costs

you want to be, and who God created you to be, and to feel safe in the process.

HEALTH CARE VERSUS SELF-CARE

Don't devalue the seed. A twenty-minute walk can do wonders for your health and mind and doesn't cost a thing. If you do the little things along the way to care for yourself, it means that you will have less drain on your assets in retirement. Caring for your health is one of the best ways to guard your assets in retirement, hands down. It is all about consistency in your self-care and in your finances, not drastic changes that don't last.

There is a saying, "People often spend their health trying to gain wealth, then people spend their wealth trying to regain their health." Don't wait to practice self-care. This is the only body you've got.

If money is coming out of your retirement assets to cover health care of some sort, I would rather you spend money on pedicures, a personal trainer, a nutritionist, or a massage therapist, rather than on doctors' visits, medication, and devices for mobility assistance. To be clear, I am grateful to have doctors and medical advancements that help us with our longevity, but we bear the greatest responsibility for our personal quality of life.

> ⅄ Genetics only account for as much as 30 percent of your longevity; most of it is how you treat the one vessel (body) you have.[28]

Consistency is key. Self-care is vital.

I want your life to be enjoyable. A great retirement planner will help you be prepared for necessary major medical interventions, but that also allows you to spend money on activities that help maintain

---

28 Genetics Home Reference, U.S. National Library of Medicine. *May 2018. "Is Longevity Determined by Genetics?"* https://ghr.nlm.nih.gov/primer/traits/longevity

your mental and physical health so you will avoid many of those major medical events in the first place.

You have likely had to handle things before. Maybe it was the family finances. Perhaps it was a work issue. Take the same approach to your well-being and health and *handle it*.

INFLATION – THE BOOGEYMAN

If longevity is the biggest risk you face in retirement, inflation is the "sidekick" that often lurks in the shadows with it. Since 1925, inflation has averaged 2.9 percent.[29] Since women tend to live longer than their male counterparts, inflation will be more impactful to a woman's retirement. Inflation erodes your future purchasing power. If you have $500,000 today, more than thirty years of inflation at 3 percent on average will reduce that $500,000 to the purchasing power of $200,000. So, your money doesn't go as far. Health care often inflates at an even quicker pace than the average cost of goods and services,[30] creating a double whammy.

You can't avoid inflation by ignoring it.

Your retirement plan needs inflation factored in to make sure it doesn't derail the future coverage you may need. We always show you how inflation could affect you in the long-term,, and then go a step further to determine your personal inflationary rate.

KIDNEY FAILURE...OR A BROKEN HEART

Met.in.africa.123@yahoo.com was the couple's email address. They were two of the most vibrant people I've ever met, and they were truly in love with each other! She was a widow from Denmark, he

---

29   Consumer Price Index. Inflation Calculator. http://www.in2013dollars.com/us/inflation/1925?amount=100
30   Alex Kacik. *Modern Healthcare. October 25, 2018. "Healthcare Price Growth Significantly Outpaces Inflation."* https://www.modernhealthcare.com/article/20181025/NEWS/181029946/healthcare-price-growth-signifi-cantly-outpaces-inflation

was a widower from the U.S. Neither expected to remarry, but they met by happenstance during a trip to Africa and fell in love. Love has a way of finding you where you least expect it.

By the time Paul and Karen came in seeking our help regarding their retirement, he was seventy-two and she was sixty-one. They were eleven years apart, just like Randy and me. The age difference endeared them to us even more. Paul was receiving daily kidney dialysis but was handling it reasonably well. Karen, on the other hand, was in exceptional health, and by all statistical accounts she would outlive her husband, possibly by many years, maybe decades.

Since they came in to seek our help when he was already receiving dialysis, there wasn't a lot of health care planning that we could do for him personally, but we wanted to create a plan for Karen. They both assumed she wouldn't need a health care plan because of her great health (an assumption many people make), so they decided against using some of their assets to create a formal long-term care plan.

- ⋏ Seven out of ten people will need to receive some form of long-term/nursing home care.[31]

- ⋏ 79 percent of employed Americans plan to continue working for wages in retirement, but only 34 percent actually do. Health-related issues are one of the primary factors that force them out of the work force before they had planned.[32]

Paul and Karen decided to self-fund any future needs, and they continued their active and energetic life.

Until the day Karen fell.

She had such a major head injury that the next time we saw her, a few months later, she was wheelchair-bound. Her vivacity had all but vanished. Paul was doing his best to keep his spirits up, and hers as

---

31 LongTermCare.gov. 2020. "How Much Care Will You Need?" https://longtermcare.acl.gov/the-basics/how-much-care-will-you-need.html
32 Employee Benefits Research Institute. 2018. "2018 EBRI Retirement Confidence Survey." https://www.ebri.org/docs/default-source/rcs/6_rcs_18-fs-2_expect.pdf?sfvrsn=e1e9302f_2

well. It was increasingly difficult to retain a smile as he attempted to care for her in his own physically compromised state. Within a couple of months, he came to the brutal realization that she needed full-time care, yet the assets they had were not enough to cover in-home care for the exhaustive nature of what she was now facing.

Paul needed outside help desperately.

Karen's children stepped in, as we often see in situations like these. Her daughter suggested that Karen move in with her, and Paul reluctantly and achingly agreed. He knew that was the best option for his wife.

One day in the fall of 2007, he drove his wife to SeaTac Airport and put her on a plane to head back to Denmark to receive care from her family.

Without him.

Because of his daily need for dialysis, Paul had to stay behind. He recognized that day was the last day he would kiss her lips or hold her hand.

The next two visits we had with Paul were gut-wrenching. Here was a seventy-five-year-old man sobbing in our office because he had lost his best friend. Because of her condition, even video conferencing via Skype or FaceTime was not a very effective way to stay in touch. He had lost his second wife, not by death, but by distance. Within six months of putting her on the plane, Paul passed away from kidney failure coupled with a broken heart.

The most difficult part about that experience, for us as planners, was that Paul and Karen had enough assets that they could have provided a level of support at home, had they approved measures we suggested before Karen's accident. The time to act is now; don't wait until it's too late.

LIKE CAR INSURANCE

Many people can't stand the thought of traditional long-term care insurance because it reminds them of car insurance. You pay these premiums for an unknown period, and then if you don't need that type of care, all that money's gone. As I've said multiple times, having control and options in retirement is paramount. I'm not a huge fan of traditional long-term care. It typically begins to get more expensive as the years progress, but there are suitable alternatives.

BETTER OPTIONS THAT RETAIN CONTROL

Often, we may look at *asset-based long-term care* or a *home health care doubler* added to an annuity.

Asset-based long-term care is an option for reasonably healthy people in their forties and fifties, and possibly early sixties. It's where you can take a chunk of assets, say for example $50,000, give it to an insurance company to purchase an annuity with an added long-term care rider (included at an additional annual cost), and if you meet certain conditions outlined in the annuity, it will provide you added funds to pay for assisted living or nursing home coverage. The annuity typically multiplies your regular income benefit by a certain amount, such as three or four times, up to a defined period, such as three to five years. If you were to die and never use the policy, the annuity's remaining value would distribute to your assigned beneficiaries rather than staying in the insurance company's pocket.

However, one constant I have seen all these years is people change their minds. Down the road, if you change your mind and want to cancel your annuity to put a down payment on a condo in Arizona (or something else fun), the insurance company often lets you add a feature that ensures you get your premium back. The insurance industry calls this a *guaranteed return of premium (ROP)* option, and you may pay an added cost for this each year. Some companies provide 100 percent ROP on day one, and others graduate it over five to seven years. Either way, it is refreshing to have options and exit strategies because no one can predict the future.

Another option is a *fixed index annuity* with a *home health care doubler* attached to the income rider. Sometimes the rider includes a fee, and sometimes it is included as a standard benefit. With this rider, if you need care—if you can no longer perform two of six *activities of daily living* (ADLs)—and your annuity usually pays out, let's say, $2,500, activating this rider means the insurance will double that amount to $5,000 per month for a set period, say three years. Every policy is different, and it is necessary to understand what the best option is for you by seeing it in conjunction with your entire retirement plan. The bottom line is that there are new and refreshing alternatives to the oppressive and unpredictable aspects of traditional long-term care policies.

You owe it to yourself to explore these options.

SHOULD I SCRAP MY CURRENT LTC POLICY?

If you have a traditional long-term care insurance policy, but you don't have a comprehensive retirement plan, you have a "micro-climate" for long-term care. You may be asking yourself whether you should continue payments on that traditional policy, especially if you receive frequent premium increases. Until you see it in the context of the entire plan, you can't answer that. Some people find the premiums to be such a drain on their fixed income, it becomes too expensive to own. Other people are right in a sweet spot.

You need to sit down with a retirement planner and see how your current long-term care coverage functions within the overall picture of your retirement plan before you make a drastic decision to drop your coverage. We're careful about recommending that you drop something you may not be able to replace. You'll want to seek expert help on this one to be totally sure of the best choice.

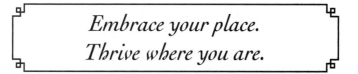

Embrace your place.
Thrive where you are.

MOST IMPORTANT TAKEAWAYS

1. Longevity is one of the most significant risks you face, often more than market risk, taxes, or inflation.

2. Right now, the largest amount of cost-shifting in history is happening with things that used to be covered by Medicare.

3. One estimation anticipates that a couple, age sixty-five, of average health, is expected to spend $285,000 on health-care-related expenses through their retirement.

4. People often spend their health trying to gain wealth, then spend their wealth trying to regain their health. Spend more of your money on healthy activities that keep you well to lessen the drain on your assets for future medical intervention.

5. Genetics account for the minority percentage of your longevity. The greatest impact is how you treat your body.

6. Seven out of ten people will need some form of long-term care.

NEXT STEPS

1. Be sure to add a little extra expense to your financial plan every month for activities that enhance your health (i.e., pedicure, massage, therapist, nutritionist).

2. Be willing to look squarely at how the cost of long-term care may derail your retirement plan. This should be a specific discussion with your planner. For married women, this is vastly important to your portfolio following your spouse's death.

3. If you are in your fifties, this is a good time to look at long-term care funding options with your planner. Your health may never be better than it is today.

4. Ask about *asset-based long-term care* or *home health care doublers* on annuity contracts as alternative options to traditional long-term care insurance.

CHAPTER 10

PROTECTION FOR THE UNEXPECTED

Stop flailing, slowing inhale, then take one step toward your destiny.

110 POUNDS OF VISCERAL FORCE

One of the absolute highlights of my role as Assistant Clinic Director of Sarvey Wildlife Care Center was getting "loved on" by a 110-pound cougar named Sasha. A tawny brown color, Sasha was stunning, graceful, playful, and powerful.

An interesting fact about cougars: They are the largest of the "small" cats, meaning they are more closely related to a domestic cat than they are to a lion or tiger. One primary distinction is they can purr. Big cats cannot. Can you imagine the deep, wonderful purr of a cat that size? It was intoxicating; you could feel it deep within your chest.

Sasha was one of our permanent residents. Someone bought her legally from a breeder in Texas, but then illegally brought her to Washington as a cub. By the time she was a juvenile at the age of eighteen months, she was too much for the owner to handle. She could get nasty at times—a commonality of "domesticated" wild animals. They may eat fancy food, wear nice collars, crave human attention, and answer to their name, but wild is still in their DNA. Sasha was no different. She needed love and affection, just like a house cat. Sasha loved to be touched but possessed the wild instincts of a deadly predator.

Her previous life of "domestication" had given her a simple trigger: children. Her old owner would let neighborhood kids come to see her, and they often poked at her through the cage bars with sticks or other instruments. The sight of children began sending her into a frenzy. It became too much for the family who kept her to control the beast within, and she landed at Sarvey, unable to be released to the wild but not safe for domestic life. Sad.

At Sarvey, volunteers would bring their children just to show them around and educate them about our wildlife operations. When they walked by Sasha's enclosure it would throw her into a fit. She'd flatten her ears against her head, bare her teeth, and lunge at the fence, growling and hissing. It was terrifying to witness. Only four people who worked at Sarvey could handle her. I was one of them.

I loved her. Sasha was my precious, beautiful girl.

Every day when she would hear me walking down the path, she would catcall to me. A massive cat "chirping" to me with excitement was a singular thrill. Her purr would kick in the moment she heard my catcall back to her, so loud you could hear it from twenty feet away. It was a wonderful bond. Because of her trust in me and the relationship I built over many years, I was in charge of cleaning her enclosure, changing her water, and removing her half-eaten carcasses. But the ultimate joy I experienced was playing games with her.

Many of the times that I went in with Sasha, I would bring a large rope toy, the kind you would use to play tug-of-war with a German Shepard or Rottweiler. We would use it the same way. Sasha would lie on the ground and we would play with this big rope, as if I was playing with an overgrown house cat. It was a blast! In my years of work with Sasha, we'd only had a handful of incidents where she had been unruly—often the result of overstimulation, her way of telling me she was done playing. Never had she been outright aggressive with me.

One warm summer day, a volunteer asked if she could come in with me and take photos of Sasha while we were playing. I had no reason to think it would be an issue and agreed.

Judy and I made our way in through the first chain-linked door to the holding area, part of a double-door of security, just in case Sasha ever made it through the first door. We got all the things ready that we were bringing in, in addition to the rope to play tug-o-war. As the first door locked behind us, I opened the second, and we made our way into Sasha's enclosure.

Sasha cat-called to me from her perch, purring like we were long-lost pals. As Judy and I entered, she jumped down and came up to rub the scent glands on the side of her cheeks on my pant leg. The second door clinked closed behind Judy, who prepared her camera, and Sasha's body tensed. She again rubbed her face against my pant leg, this time aggressively, then swung her mouth around to bite down hard on my right thigh.

Something had changed.

As I tried to regain control of the deadly predator that weighed only twenty pounds less than me, Judy screamed. Sasha let go of my leg and lunged again, wrapping her powerful front paws around my waist and sinking her razor-sharp teeth into the left side of my chest, then the right side. She then dropped back to all fours before clamping down onto my left thigh.

Judy panicked, and I was terrified Sasha would go for her.

I was utterly shocked at how fast it went from bad to worse, awed by the sheer flexibility and speed of a cat like that. If she hadn't been declawed on her front paws, I would have been vastly outmatched that day.

Still screaming, Judy escaped the enclosure, leaving me to defend myself. I shoved my left hand into Sasha's mouth, grabbed her throat with my right hand, and kneed her in the chest over and over. She moaned, and hissed, and finally let go, allowing me to leave.

Allowing me to leave.

The moment the door closed behind me, Sasha was back up to the side of the enclosure purring as if we were long lost friends, as though nothing had happened. I've had domestic cats all my life, and it was reminiscent of their bizarre behaviors. One moment you're relaxed, petting them, and the next, they bite your hand, flicking their back legs and claws all over your unprotected arm, leaving some nasty scratches as they run off.

Imagine that pet cat at ten times the weight.

Severe maiming or damage was not part of my story that day, but it wasn't due to luck. Avoiding a serious injury was a result of planning and preparation for the unknown.

It was a seventy-five-degree day in July, but I was still wearing jeans and a heavy denim jacket with wool lining on the inside. I received pressure wounds on both sides of my chest and thighs, but nothing broke the surface in those areas because I had the right protection for the job. I suffered a one-inch gash on the hand I had thrust in her mouth, but that was the only part of my body fully exposed. Thank God. If Sasha had wanted to really hurt me, she could have chomped down on my hand, breaking every bone in it. That was never her intention. She loved me, but she was still wild.

I cared very deeply for this wonderfully confused animal, torn between being wild and wanting to be touched, played with, and petted. Yet I knew Sasha was wild down to her bones and never to be taken for granted, so I always went in with the proper attire, prepared for the unknown.

PREPARE FOR THE UNKNOWN

Individuals face unknowns in retirement all the time. Those corrections could include market corrections, the premature death of a spouse, or long-term health care needs. We see it every day. People want to hope for the best (and we do, too), but they often avoid planning for the worst.

When life comes at you like an angry cougar, you *can* be prepared and make it through with little harm. You may suffer from minor discomfort, but you can recover.

PROTECTING WHAT MATTERS MOST — WHITE PICKET FENCE

Most people think life insurance, even the cheapest kind (term insurance), is only for those who have young kids or a mortgage. In many minds, it acts as the white picket fence around those things and people that matter most.

That's not untrue, but life insurance can also be a lot more.

Insurance is, at its foundation, always going to be about the death benefit, sure. But there are now some very sophisticated products that also provide benefits like cash savings, tax strategies, charitable giving opportunities, long-term care funding, and on and on. We love to use these different kinds of policies within the broad context of an overall plan to provide advantages for our clients.

One commonality is that insurance costs and policy lengths always vary based on the insured's health, a factor that can change rapidly and alter or eliminate your chances of coverage. That's why it's incredibly important to have this conversation with your financial planner sooner rather than later. Remember, lack of planning is still a plan.

CHEAP IS NOT ALWAYS A BAD THING

You may benefit from an inexpensive ten- or twenty-year term insurance policy on your spouse. If they die prematurely, that kind of policy can ensure you are not left without proper assets to last the rest of your life. The premium never goes up, but like car insurance, if that person doesn't die within that time period, those premiums are gone for good. Not ideal, but still better than if they die prematurely and you are left with insufficient resources.

Every time we sit down with potential clients, we show what it looks like if your spouse dies early in retirement.

If you are single, the same may apply for the protection of your heirs. Life insurance may provide the ability to slowly and systematically handle the settling of your estate upon your passing. This is far more advantageous than heirs rushing to sell your home or liquidating IRAs to pay your tax bill within the allotted nine months required. Many kids must rush to sell their parents' house, which puts a ton of pressure on them to get it emptied and ready to sell. The market may not be in the best position to facilitate a favorable sale.

Life insurance proceeds give beneficiaries tax-free money to pay tax bills and final expenses for funerals and memorials. Such proceeds allow them time to mourn instead of immediately having to confront a financial calamity while grieving. I am not saying that you have created a situation like that, but you must openly discuss what your death will mean for your heirs or how, if you are married, your spouse's death will impact you.

WHO'S PREPARED FOR ANOTHER GREAT RECESSION OR CORONAVIRUS BLACK SWAN EVENT?

Me! If you can't say that, the question back would be, "Why?"

Having learned a number of financial lessons in 2008, Randy and I were not going to make those same mistakes if we hit another difficult time. It appears from my vantage point at coronavirus "ground zero" in my hometown of Kirkland that we are in for a rough ride, and financial markets are *very* unhappy. Some are speaking the "D-word"… yikes…a depression. We constantly discuss the possibility of a major correction with our staff and clients. You *can* adequately plan for the unknown, and it appears we are smack dab in the middle of it. A company can plan for the worst, and so can an individual. But we are not fazed, we are ready to handle it, and feeling prepared and confident feels much better than the alternative. You deserve to feel that way and should be able to if you take responsibility and have an adviser who has "seen some things" in their career.

As a company, we walked our clients through the "dot-bomb" of the early millennium and the Great Recession. Great planning is not hard to do, but you need help from those who have gone before you and have walked that path. You need to know the proper "attire" to protect yourself, in the form of solid planning that looks closely at market risk (Chapter Seven) and how much you could lose in another event like that.

Health care, market risk, and longevity are the three biggest what-ifs in retirement. Let's make sure you have clear answers to all of these. Let's handle it together. Your loved ones will be forever grateful for your foresight.

> *Consistency is the driving factor that dictates the trajectory of your life.*

MOST IMPORTANT TAKEAWAYS

1. Hope for the best but plan for the worst.

2. Lack of planning is a foolish plan. Don't procrastinate.

3. Insurance may be a strong addition to your legacy for your heirs.

4. Inexpensive term insurance may give you the assurance that you need to walk through the next twenty years.

NEXT STEPS

1. Ask your adviser to show you what your retirement plan looks like if your spouse dies prematurely. You should be able to see if that causes you to run out of money before age 100.

2. Health dictates whether you can qualify for most insurance, so you need to confront this shortly after your team has devised your retirement plan. At your next appointment, ask your adviser to show you if insurance would be of benefit and start "shopping" for it while your health is still good.

3. Get educated on the different types of insurance offered and how those may benefit you and your family.

CHAPTER 11

WHY HIRE AN ADVISER?

> *The separation is in the*
> *preparation; get to work.*

THE ARTIST AND THE ENGINEER:
INITIAL VISIT

When Earnest and Laura came into our office, our appointment began with an out-of-the-ordinary greeting. Laura saw me, got all giddy and excited like I was a celebrity, hugged me tight, and told me how excited she was to be in our office, and that she couldn't believe they got to meet with *me* (likely because I can't meet with everyone who needs help and I mention that at my seminars). I ushered them into the conference room where their specialty coffees and our yummy treat plate awaited them. After a few moments of pleasantries, she sat down at the table and said directly to me, "He handles everything." She then proceeded to stare off in the distance out the window.

Uh, okay, I thought.

Her husband walked by and sat down in his seat beside her. As I made my way around the table to sit down across from them and to begin some small talk, he launched right in and said, "I have nearly $500,000 in a 401(k) still at my former employer. I want to talk about investing it in a fixed index annuity." I was taken aback by how direct he was, and I knew most financial advisers would instantly have jumped in to address him specifically regarding his request.

But to his slight frustration and disappointment, I didn't.

"You know, I apologize, Earnest, but I really need to ask some questions before we get into any of that discussion. To be honest with you, I won't get into that at this visit and probably won't get into that discussion at the next visit, either," I said. "It's important for me, as a fiduciary, to make sure I'm doing what's in your best interest, and it's also very important for the protection of my licensure to make sure that I'm giving the proper recommendation. That would be like you going to the doctor and telling them in the first thirty seconds that you want them to prescribe Percocet before they've looked over your medical records or done a physical. That can get me in a whole lot of trouble." I smiled.

He smiled back and nodded in agreement.

"It's important that I look at your overall financial picture and how it all functions together before I make that recommendation." I then looked over at Laura, who was still staring out the window, and said, "but I think that will also be really helpful for you." I pointed to his wife and looked her right in the eyes. She looked startled and had this look that said, "I can't believe she's talking to me."

Yep, I am talking to you too. Your opinions and thoughts matter!

We went through our Initial Visit process. It always consists of four elements:

1. Finding out why someone has decided to take fifty minutes out of their life to meet with someone in our office; what concerns or questions are at the forefront of their minds.

2. Expressing clearly who we are as a company, sharing our philosophy.

3. Discussing their values and what they perceive to be their perfect day (the things they really want to be doing besides working or counting their money).

4. Beginning to get a general sense of their current financial situation so we can build them a retirement plan at our next strategy visit.

As we began to talk about what was on Earnest's mind other than the 401(k) at his former employer, he really didn't have much to discuss. "What about you, Laura? Is there anything that you are concerned about regarding your retirement or current financial picture?" She smiled and shook her head. I asked a few more probing questions, and when I asked about the long-term view…the floodgates opened.

"Everyone in your family dies before they reach seventy. You're sixty-eight," Laura leveled at Earnest.

"My last physical was fine," he responded.

"You don't eat well," Laura quipped.

"I'm healthy as an ox," Earnest pushed back.

Their banter became rather comical, but it was clear they were reaching the heart of a chasm in their communication, a void that had gone unfilled for years. Earnest was a caring, loving spouse. He had worked hard to care for his family and wife and had largely succeeded. Yet, when Laura hinted at her deep and growing fear of being left alone, exposed, he was quick to say, "Honey, we are fine, we have enough money." But his pacifying response to her didn't cut it.

In black-and-white, she'd never seen what the actual evidence was to support a resolution to the question, "Will I be okay?" And Earnest wasn't the most qualified to address that—most of us struggle somewhat with the concrete reality of what the world might look like once we are no longer in it. For years, she had been barely keeping a lid on a mounting sense of panic.

After fifty minutes, we concluded our visit and scheduled our Strategy Visit (second meeting). I had plenty of information to build a plan showing them where they currently were, *YOU ARE HERE*, and they only needed to supply me with their investment statements from their brokerage accounts. They agreed to get me those in the next few days prior to our next visit.

STRATEGY VISIT

A week had passed, and Earnest and Laura were back in the office to see me. We headed back into one of our conference rooms and enjoyed some brief conversation. I asked if anything had changed, then re-read my notes from the Initial Visit. I also took a moment to remind them of our Strategy Visit process:

1. Walk through the first view of their current retirement plan with conservative, yet reasonable, projections for rates of return for all their investments, with absolutely no changes or additions— YOU ARE HERE.

2. Mention and note any concerns or issues we see at first blush.

3. Walk through our risk assessment software, the risk and fee analysis of their household, and help them through the risk tolerance test, as a couple.

4. If they want our help after all these steps, we will talk about how we engage in a working relationship.

We were all back on the same page.

I launched our retirement planning software on the TV screen to walk them through the first picture of their retirement, and when Laura saw it, her whole body language changed. She sat up tall, turned her entire body, and fully faced the TV, watching intently. You could see she was taking it in like a kid seeing snow for the first time. When we got to the end of it, she pointed at the screen and said loud and directly, "That! That, whatever *that* is, I get it!" That was one of the highlight moments of my entire career. At that moment, I saw a disengaged woman realize she could understand her financial picture after forty-two years of marriage.

It was awesome!

When she saw that our retirement planning software could distill her entire financial picture in a way *she* comprehended, without the distractions of the specifics and the intricacies that her husband enjoyed, you could see a woman becoming empowered and starting to feel safe. She began to pull her head out of the sand and appreciate all her husband had done. All Laura needed was to see the big picture that told her the money they saved over all these years could be enough to take her through retirement, take them both through any health care events, and let them live the retirement of their dreams!

I looked at her and said, "Well, my dear, spoiler alert, you actually have more than enough money. By the time you're in your eighties, you should still have a fair sum remaining." She had a look of shock on her face, but then seemed to get a little squeamish. "I don't want to die with so much money left over," she said. Then she paused with a glare in her eyes, looked at her husband, then looked back at me and asked, "Then why was Earnest so frugal all these years?" I cautiously chuckled and said, "That's something you'll have to talk about with him. Maybe that's why you're where you're at."

It was amusing to watch, but it spoke volumes about her lack of understanding of their "big picture."

By the end of the second visit, she had a *Best Life Retirement Plan* that showed her their basic account values and what companies held what. We had discussed whether or not they were at risk of running out of money, and how all of their assets could work together with his pension, both of their Social Security benefits, inflation, and taxes. Their investments didn't tell her all on their own that she would be cared for in her eighties if he died and she needed long-term care. That is the purpose of having a written plan.

The comprehensive financial plan we constructed for Laura and Earnest seemed eye-opening, especially for her. When she was holding it in her hands, caressing the edges of the pages between her fingers, you would think that she was holding and rubbing something made of gold. She was touching "financial clarity" for the first time with amazement and awe. Laura finally realized the results of her husband's years of work and care for their finances. His years of saving had paid off, and she now felt that she would be taken care of for the rest of her life.

That realization is the *huge* difference between investing and retirement planning.

STRATEGY VISIT NO. 2

We don't always have a second Strategy Visit, but Earnest and Laura wanted more information before continuing the process, and our process can certainly accommodate that. The two arrived separately and, as Earnest and I waited for Laura's arrival, I figured he'd want to launch into the crux of his very first question about fixed index annuities, so I prepared my discussion points, but he stopped me.

"Before we get started, I wanted to tell you how grateful I am for what you did for my wife. It meant so much to her to see things the way they were laid out, and it meant a lot to me, too. She left that last meeting so happy."

Seeing a woman go from having never understood her financial picture to having clarity and peace of mind about the future of herself and her husband was a major touchstone of my career.

What is crazier is that this conversation came after the second visit. It came after she was able to see the first collective snapshot of all that she and her husband owned. This holistic look at their retirement accounts combined all those micro-climates into one, and it made all the difference. Earnest and Laura never became clients—Earnest thoroughly enjoyed managing their money, and he wasn't willing to give that up yet—but I think of them just about every time a couple comes in, wondering if they need to hear the same thing Laura did.

As I say in our initial visit and at seminars, "The Strategy Visit will be the most valuable visit you have with us, and most people who get through that don't become clients for one reason or another. Might be timing, money is inaccessible, or any number of other reasons. But our mission is to leave you better than when you came in. Seeing where you currently stand is the most powerful part of our work, whether you become our client or not."

Randy and I have been told over the years that we have saved marriages. This is confirmation that the work we do as financial advisers and retirement planners is more than just handling people's money. It's like being a money therapist.

Even the best savers and investors can't always bridge the gap with the person they love the most, their spouse or partner, or they can't "get past themselves." We help singles get through that roadblock, too. That is just one part of the significant work we do for our clients *and* prospective clients who never engage us. It is solid, meaningful work, and we love it!

SAVE ME FROM MY KIDS

"My daughter is mad because I won't give her some money," Linda told me after coming in for a visit, then began to tear up.

She also mentioned she had just received a final payout for a piece of property that was in her family. The proceeds were split between her and her ex-husband. She divorced in her early sixties and was nearing seventy. The $110,000 she received from the sale was going to be exactly what she needed to fulfill the remaining long-term goals of her retirement.

Unfortunately, her daughter also found out about it and began to put the hard press on her mom to give her some money. Her daughter was self-sufficient, as one generally ought to be by their mid-forties, but had been quite upset that she hadn't gotten what she saw as "her share."

Linda was looking for confirmation she did the right thing, even though she felt terrible about it inside. After we plugged everything into her retirement plan, it showed very clearly that she absolutely needed that money for the overall health of her retirement and future health care planning. Shaving off $30,000 or $40,000 of those proceeds would diminish the long-term viability of her plan. She was able to see the negative effect herself as we simulated that "alternate plan," which was more powerful than me just telling her it wasn't a good idea.

As tears welled up in her eyes, I kept reiterating she did the right thing, and that her daughter would benefit better in the long run by not having to become a caregiver if her mother ever had long-term health issues. Sometimes we need to hear it multiple times to know that we made the right decision. Ultimately, she took my advice and continued to stand strong and retain the money in her investment accounts. Way to go, Mama!

These are the typical stories that go on day after day in people's lives—grown children who haven't figured out how to take care of themselves and are still needing to rely on Mom or Dad—and usually the requests fall on Mom. We need to know what we have in terms of money and then see clearly how our choices might play out. We need to have a clear plan; it makes decisions like this much simpler, but not easy.

Stay strong, ladies! You need and deserve to feel secure.

WHAT GOT YOU THERE WON'T KEEP YOU THERE

I am a lifelong athlete.

I began as a competitive swimmer at the age of seven, burning out by the end of sixth grade with six practices a week. I was done with swimming, but I was just getting started on athletics and wanted to try all that I could while I could. I dabbled in gymnastics but soon grew taller than the instructor. I excelled in basketball, softball, and track. But the sport that truly won my heart was volleyball. The teamwork, finesse, and aggressiveness drew me in. Spiking a ball in someone's face was often a terrifically satisfying experience, and I took a devious pleasure in seeing my opponents wince.

The first time I played volleyball was in seventh grade. I was hooked. My mom worked weekends to pay for me to play year-round. Through school, I also played the other sports—for fun, of course. Volleyball took me to be a Division I athlete at the University of Washington.

Obviously, I knew how to do the "sports thing." Until I decided to run my first half-marathon.

I am built to be a sprinter. All of the sports I played required short bursts of energy. In volleyball, we'd pass a ball back and forth over a net until it hit the ground. Rest, reset, and do it again. In track, I'd run the 100- or 200-meter hurdles or compete in the long jump. The events required twenty seconds or less of explosive energy, rest, reset, and do it one or two more times. In swimming, I rarely swam more than a 200-meter race. Usually, I competed in the 50- or 100-meter freestyle or butterfly. The events took less than sixty seconds, then hours of rest until the next race.

When I accepted a friend's challenge to run a half-marathon, I had no idea how much different that would be from all my other training. Many people were not surprised I committed to the challenge. "You're built for that stuff. It'll be easy for you!" some said.

How misinformed they were.

Training for distance is wildly different from sprinting and short-distance work. It required me to think entirely differently about how I ate, when I ran, how often I ran, and what my recovery was. My lungs and limbs were not ready for this type of work. I was hurting myself trying to prepare, and I wasn't seeing the kind of performance that told me I could make it. That was, until I hired a coach who laid out a simple, easy-to-follow plan that was uniquely suited to distance running.

This is what I often see with individuals who have done a great job accumulating wealth. Maybe you did it yourself. Or you hired an adviser who specializes in growing, saving, and accumulating wealth. Even though I had great coaches in years gone by, their direction about how to prepare myself for volleyball, softball, swimming, or short-distance races in track didn't help me in preparing to run a half-marathon. It doesn't matter that my weightlifting coach at UW set the national record for the squat in his age bracket. That type of coach was not going to equip me for my first half-marathon, but my trainer who ran IRONMAN® triathlons would.

Accumulating assets while in your twenties, thirties, and forties requires one set of skills. But when you approach retirement and the time in which you are nearing *decumulation,* this stage of the journey requires a totally new set of skills. What got you there will not automatically keep you there.

Let me repeat: What got you there might not keep you there.

PEDIATRICIAN AT 55?

If you remained with the adviser who helped you save all that money for the last twenty years, it might be like going to the kindest, friendliest, most world-class pediatrician all your life, and expecting him to be the right doctor for you when you hit fifty-five. I don't care how amazing, nice, skilled, good-looking, or knowledgeable he is; his area of expertise is treating children. Period.

You need to hire a retirement planner who specializes in helping you protect your assets, income planning, risk-managed growth, RMD tax integration, and health care planning. Not only should they be knowledgeable about these areas, but they should also have a personality and attitude that meshes well with yours—ideally, they will be working with you for a long time. If you do this part of your life wrong because you think you "got it handled" or decide to skimp on quality coaching because you're being cheap, you could damage your future in one 2008-esque event. Just like I could have ruined my knees, ankles, and body beyond repair training inappropriately for a half-marathon. You have only one body. And you have only one chance at retiring the right way.

Seasons of life change and the coaches you need along the way ought to change along with you.

ESSENCE OF WORKING WITH AN INDEPENDENT FIDUCIARY

"Is there a way my twenty-two-year-old can get temporary car insurance on our less expensive vehicle?"

As our oldest son, Morgan, graduated and returned home to Seattle from college in Phoenix, we realized he needed to be able to use one of our cars from time to time. His main ride, a motorcycle, wasn't going to be as exciting in the Seattle winter, but until he sold it and got his own car, we wanted to be sure we were appropriately covered.

We reached out to our Allstate agent. We learned we could put him on our policy, but that required Morgan to be covered on both our vehicles, which are much nicer than a new college grad would ideally drive. When they told us it would cost $224 per month to add him, I nearly fell out of my chair. What?! *Why*?! Allstate said that was the only way to do it, by fully adding him to our policy (and both vehicles). So, I decided to reach out to an insurance broker that had more than just Allstate products to offer.

I called the broker and asked her about options for our son. She said it was simple: We could get a "non-owner" insurance policy. That would give him coverage to drive any of our cars, or a friend's car. The cost was $79 per month. What? How can that be? I asked the next logical question: "Why didn't Allstate offer me that?" Well, come to find out, they can't because they don't have access to that type of policy. It isn't in their menu of offerings.

Grrrrr. That's not right.

She described the very significant difference between working with a proprietary company like Allstate, which only offers Allstate products, versus a broker who can offer any line of insurance from a myriad of companies. The broker had the whole world of insurance options available to meet our specific needs, as opposed to Allstate, which provides fewer options and just gave me the best of the options they had.

I learned a valuable lesson that day as we obtained insurance for Morgan at $79 per month. We also found a new auto insurance provider.

That is the essence of working with an independent fiduciary.

A fiduciary is someone who is entrusted with the care of money or property and who has a legal obligation to act in the best interest of another.

Being a fiduciary is very important to me. It holds me to a higher standard of care for my clients. It also allows me to truly offer what I believe is best for each unique situation I encounter. I believe this should be a determining factor with any adviser you work with. I will also take it a step further to say you don't just want any fiduciary, but an independent one, one who isn't just limited to the products that are pushed by their parent company.

Allstate, or Geico, or Progressive are the car insurance equivalent of many well-intentioned financial firms that offer only a certain range of products or investments. The advisers or agents who work for them are going to offer you the "best" of what they have, but what if some other company down the street has an even better product, but they can't offer that to you? Independent fiduciaries have a wider range of products they can recommend and can offer more customized products and advice.

So, it is very simple. Ask your adviser, "Are you independent, and are you a fiduciary?" If the answer is "No," you will want to think hard about the continuation of that relationship.

DON'T STOP AT ONE

Interview a few advisers when searching for one. Just like selecting a doctor, you want to make sure you can communicate easily, that you feel you can speak openly without fear of rejection, ridicule, or judgment, and that you just get a good sense being around that individual. Talk to the adviser's team too. You can find out a lot about parents by speaking to their kids, and the same goes for team members who work for the adviser. Since solid planning takes a great team, you will often be working with support staff along your journey, just like a nurse or receptionist at a doctor's office. Make sure you like the whole package. Otherwise, keep looking.

Do your research, ask for references (yes, you can do that), and then trust your intuition. Women's intuition is often right, even if you can't explain it.

> *Back to basics: fundamentals and execution. They may not be sexy, but they'll help you win the race.*

MOST IMPORTANT TAKEAWAYS

1. There is a big difference between investment and retirement planning.

2. You need to be coachable to change. What got you there won't necessarily keep you there.

3. Don't let grown kids dictate your future security. You earned this time to be selfish.

4. Hire an independent fiduciary.

5. Trust your gut and ask for references.

NEXT STEPS

1. Say out loud, "I am coachable and willing to change. I provide value for many people. I deserve a sound financial plan for my life."

2. Get a written plan. Reach out this week to your adviser to build you a comprehensive view of what you currently own. YOU ARE HERE.

3. Pick up your phone or shoot off a quick email asking your current adviser if they are a fiduciary. You have every right to probe. If they aren't, seriously consider a change and begin interviewing others.

CHAPTER 12

GETTING STARTED & ORGANIZED

> *Just take one step. That may be*
> *your greatest success today.*

I DON'T WANT TO WASTE YOUR TIME

"You know, Arwen, I didn't schedule an initial visit." As I stood at the door of the venue following the conclusion of my seminar, I politely thanked Valerie for telling me. Then she continued. "Well, let me tell you why. I just didn't want to waste your time. I got divorced about three years ago. I'm fifty-five years old. My ex-husband left me with a mountain of debt, and I don't think I'm ever going to be able to retire."

As she took a breath to continue with her excuses for not scheduling a visit with me, I interjected. "You know what, just come in," I said. "Let's sit and visit about your situation, because my job is to provide you *hope*."

So, she took me up on the offer and scheduled an initial visit.

When Valerie came in, we talked about her concerns, enjoyed some time talking about her values and her "perfect day" (what she really enjoys doing when she gets to do what she wants), and then gathered specifics about her situation. She actually had the pieces of a great retirement; she just didn't know it yet. I gathered the necessary information and, as our time concluded, I scheduled her next visit, the Strategy Visit, with one of our other advisers. I reiterated that we at Becker Retirement Group work as a team, and he would be a great fit for her personality and be able to walk her through her first view of her comprehensive retirement plan. She was eager and looking forward to it.

When she arrived for her next visit, they shared a few pleasantries and then he read her an overview of my copious notes to make sure I had evaluated her situation correctly. Up on the TV, he began to walk page by page through the YOU ARE HERE version of her *Best Life Retirement Plan*. When he got to the retirement page after plugging in all her assets, income, and expenses (including the debt), you should have seen the look of disbelief on her face at how far she had come, and where she would go if she just persisted.

Even in a short period, she was surprised at how much she was *handling it*. We just provided her confirmation and evidence she could see and touch.

This wasn't through any planning we had yet done. Her confidence was in finally seeing all of her financial assets in one place, and how they all worked together, no more micro-climates. This is why the second visit (Strategy Visit) is the most valuable visit we have with anyone, whether they become a client or not.

Tears welled in her eyes. She was so shocked and floored.

After a bit more discussion that day, he printed her *Best Life Retirement Plan* and handed it to her. Then she said, while looking through it and caressing the pages, "Oooh, wow, is this mine? Thank you! Okay, so how do we start working together?"

There was a pause before he answered.

"You know Valerie, to be honest with you, at this point, you seem to be on a pretty good path of accumulating what you'll need in retirement. There's not much we could do that would add to your situation currently since you are only fifty-five and all your money is being saved in your 401(k) at work. Why don't you take your *Best Life Retirement Plan*, and think about us when you're nearing fifty-nine-and-a-half or if you happen to retire from this company early?"

She was a bit deflated that she wasn't starting to work with our firm, but was content. You could see her exhale as she saw her retirement picture more clearly.

Then her look shifted to a possible "sticker shock." While holding her *Best Life Retirement Plan* out towards our adviser, she inquired, "Well, how much do I pay you for this?"

He responded, "Nothing. We actually don't charge anything during these phases of our retirement planning process." She grabbed his hands and gave him the biggest "thank you" hug.

A great adviser, male or female, will be able to provide direction, guidance, and, ultimately, *hope*.

HOW CAN BECKER RETIREMENT GROUP PROVIDE YOU HOPE?

At Becker Retirement Group, one thing I strive to do is leave you better than when you came in. That is the mantra our team lives by, and we could do that for you. That's our number one goal and, quite honestly, our only goal.

IN PERSON

When you come into any of our offices around the Puget Sound area, you are first greeted by our terrific team and offered a yummy drink menu. The menu has all sorts of coffees, flavored waters, teas, sodas, hot chocolate, anything that you would really want (except for the tequila, that is only late in the day on Fridays...haha...just kidding).

While sipping on a soothing beverage, you might be lounging on the couch, watching some of our funny or educational videos, hearing a bit of our radio show, or enjoying some of the hilarious pictures from the myriad client events we throw throughout the year. Then, when you come into one of our meeting rooms, there's a treat plate waiting for you. It has these amazing cinnamon cookies, dried mangos, delightful warm nuts, and Boehm's chocolates, handmade especially for us.

ONLINE AND OVER THE PHONE

If you live out of the area, we are still here to help. Having been in business for more than twenty years as Becker Retirement Group (Randy's experience in the industry exceeds thirty years), we have clients who live all over the country. They include snowbirds longing for the desert heat of Arizona, clients who move to the sunny skies of Florida, or those who moved back to be near their extended family in Illinois. Our planning and conversations don't stop at that point. We just alter the way we communicate (and we became exceptional at this type of interface after all the additional practice through the COVID-19 "shelter in place" mandate). We will get on the phone and have a brief fifteen-minute phone call to see if an online "screen" visit will be beneficial for you, then we will schedule our Initial Visit.

Whether over the phone or in-person for the Initial Visit, we are just going to chat. It is very low-key. That is why it is called a visit. We're going to talk a little bit about what's keeping you up at night or what's on your mind as it relates to your specific situation, and why you carved fifty minutes out of your life to meet with us. Then we will fill in a bit more about who we are as a company, our history, and we'll talk about your core values. We ask for you to imagine your "perfect day." Finally, we ask a handful of questions about the specifics and details of your financial situation.

This initial visit costs nothing (except fifty minutes *very well* spent) and, if that's something that you are considering, I think that's a tremendous blessing for you and your peace of mind. We never charge any fees for any of our visits, now or twenty years in the future.

We also don't charge for the creation of a *Best Life Retirement Plan*.

When Randy founded the company in September 1999, he decided against imposing a charge to create comprehensive financial plans for our prospective clients. Many of our friends and counterparts charge $1,500 for a comprehensive financial plan like our *Best Life Retirement Plan*, but we don't. We haven't since our inception, and I don't imagine we are ever going to charge for them. We are happy to provide that service at no cost.

WE AREN'T A NOT-FOR-PROFIT COMPANY

"So, if you don't charge for the creation of the comprehensive financial plan, how do you get paid?"

Great question!

Most of the individuals who walk through our door do not become clients. That could be for any number of reasons—the timing isn't right, assets are tied up and inaccessible, someone favors their current financial adviser, or they love managing their own money. The list goes on and on, but occasionally the fit is perfect.

At the Strategy Visit, we complete the first draft of your *Best Life Retirement Plan* (YOU ARE HERE). You get to see what concerns we outline. We see how we feel we can make a meaningful *positive* impact on your life, and you want us to help you solve issues we uncovered.

Following the Strategy Visit, we lay out our initial plan and how we are compensated. It might be by managing your assets and charging an advisory fee, or through introducing other financial tools and insurance products for which the insurance company compensates us directly with commissions.

Most of our clients have a blend of both managed money and guaranteed funds, but ultimately everyone's situation is unique.

Once your plan is underway, we discuss long-term care, insurance, and future tax planning, and we review both your plan and risk posture annually.

BUT I ALREADY HAVE A FINANCIAL ADVISER

Most of the people we sit down with have a financial adviser. You might even have two or three financial advisers. That's okay. It's common because we go through different seasons of our financial lives. I can recall my first softball coach, my second volleyball coach, and my first two weightlifting coaches as some of the best coaches in my life. But they could not prepare me for my first half-marathon. They each specialized in other areas of athletic development.

Your current adviser may specialize in accumulation of wealth: growing, saving, and adjusting to situations people confront in their twenties, thirties, and forties. But when you start transitioning into your late fifties, sixties, seventies, and beyond, many unique pieces must be addressed for that season of life. I believe that you want to be talking to somebody who is an independent fiduciary and somebody who specializes in retirement planning, and who can coordinate your finances with tax planning.

After getting divorced at twenty-four, I had to take time to rebuild—time that I had. At sixty-five, however, we don't have the time or luxury to make big financial mistakes. You might have just one chance to get it right, and that chance is happening now.

I'M MARRIED; WHAT ABOUT MY SPOUSE?

Married ladies could be thinking, "Well, my spouse isn't reading this. I don't know if *they'll want* to come in with me. I don't know if *I want* them to come in with me." We actually hear that often. It's all right to have the Initial Visit by yourself if you want or need to. Sometimes women have questions they would rather ask on their own.

With just one of you at the Initial Visit, we can get a clear framework of who you are, what matters to you, and where you stand. The meeting will give you enough of a feeling about us to know if you want to proceed for another visit. Usually we have enough information to start building out the initial *Best Life Retirement Plan*. We will need your spouse or partner at the Strategy Visit so they can help fill in gaps and make sure the plan is clear, concise, and accurate (this is also vital if you want to keep your marriage strong financially and do planning as a team).

Fidelity Investments conducted a study that showed couples who had a dedicated adviser were more likely to agree that it wasn't hard to talk about money compared to those who didn't.[33] If you see yourself and your spouse in that statistic, please don't allow confusion or potential resistance from your spouse to stop you from making forward progress. Your future well-being and peace of mind is more important than the discomfort of a confrontation. Many marriage fights are about money, but bringing in a "money therapist" (a.k.a. a retirement planner) can help you settle some of those unknowns that cause fear and anxiety between spouses, and help bridge the gap between how you and your spouse see things.

Be willing to question your current situation. Your future self will thank you for it. Get out there, sister, and handle it!

---

33 Fidelity. 2018. "2018 Fidelity Investments Couples & Money Study." https://www.fidelity.com/bin-public/060_www_fidelity_com/documents/pr/couples-fact-sheet.pdf

> *Consistency and commitment are constant traits in a successful and meaningful life.*

MOST IMPORTANT TAKEAWAYS

1. Meeting with a retirement planner is designed to provide *hope* and *clarity* related to your current direction.

2. We can work with you in person or over the phone / computer.

3. If your financial adviser isn't one that *specializes* in retirement planning, it may be time to look around for one who is an independent fiduciary and does.

4. It is okay to question your spouse and take the lead at getting outside help from a professional. Even if your spouse isn't "on board" when you start the process, you may be pleasantly surprised to see them come around after holding a clear plan in their hands.

NEXT STEP

1. Start today! Schedule a time with a few planners to see if they have the capability to do all the things we have talked about. There are thousands of tremendous, caring advisers who can do all that I have mentioned for you. Keep looking until you find one *and* you like how they communicate. This relationship may last ten, twenty, or more years, so be diligent and get what *you* want and need.

CONCLUSION

Refuse to live a life of regret.

You know what you need to do; now you just need to start. No one is going to do this for you. There is no knight in shining armor to save you from all your hurt and struggle. The pot o' gold doesn't exist at the end of the beautiful rainbow. You'll always be left grasping for air. It is all an illusion to keep you stuck. You aren't drinking this Kool-Aid. Your eyes are open.

"I'm gonna handle this." Say it out loud. *I'm gonna handle this.* I've got this. I am worthy and able. I am a highly capable woman. I am learning more every day. I matter to many people. I will handle this. My time is now. No more indecision. I am doing this!

The planning you do today isn't just about you—it's about the generations to come.

Pick up the phone. Make the call. Do the research. Take financial inventory. Interview some advisers. Talk to people you look up to in the area of finance. Get direction and start moving. God can only direct you when you are moving, not when you are standing still. Move; even if it ends up being the wrong direction, you will get set on the right path!

This is just the beginning of something amazing and miraculous. You are a part of something bigger than yourself. You are part of a movement. A movement of women and ladies who are not willing to sit back and let someone else dictate their lives. Women who won't allow an industry to tell them how they need to learn and where they best find their place in all this. Who don't believe the lies saying they are flaky or indecisive. Women who refuse to agree that understanding personal finance is a "man's job" because the industry struggles to pivot and speak to the real players—you.

Women. Mothers. Daughters. Sisters. Aunts. Nieces. The last woman standing. You.

You ready for this new game? I've got your back.

Look at you, transitioning into your destiny. Not a little wallflower, but a bad-ass chick! I'm so proud of you. You did what I knew you would.

You handled it!

ABOUT THE AUTHOR

Arwen Becker is a Financial Adviser, National Speaker, Author, Host of the She Handled It! Podcast and Co-Owner of Becker Retirement Group in Bellevue, Washington. Alongside her husband, Randy Becker (the other Co-Owner of Becker Retirement Group), she has spent more than twenty years in the financial industry.

As an Investment Adviser Representative, Arwen has the sole motivation of leaving people better than she found them. Over the years, she has discovered a very common thread, that women are experts at handling it when life get messy. When things go sideways, women sacrifice time, energy, and money to handle it, often to their own detriment. Financial education often takes a back seat since women are busy doing things that truly matter, caring for people they love. After speaking with thousands of ladies over the years, she has made it Becker Retirement Group's mission to help connect with women in her community who aren't getting the attention and help they need and truly deserve.

Additionally, Arwen has taken a direct focus on changing the way women are served by the financial industry and leaders by launching her training organization, LIFE with Arwen. LIFE (Leaders Inspiring Female Empowerment) is devoted to leading companies and individuals to reach, inspire, and impact the women they employ or serve in the area of life and money, and to better understand how women learn differently. Arwen walks through money issues facing women today, lessons that are simple and executable in every stage of their financial journeys...truly taking the conversation of money from the head to the heart.

Arwen, with her husband, Randy, is an adoring parent of three incredible boys, and she takes pleasure in traveling, crafting, serving her local church, and enjoying the family cabin on Harstine Island. Arwen is a lifelong athlete, currently enjoying early morning runs and long day hikes with her family and friends.

To book Arwen as your organization's featured speaker, visit **www.LIFEwithArwen.com**

Becker Retirement Group Website: **www.BeckerRetirement.com**

Facebook: **@LIFEwithArwen**

Instagram: **@ArwenBecker**

LinkedIn: **@ArwenBecker**

iTunes/Spotify: *She Handled It!* **Podcast**

SPECIAL THANKS

To Bill Kentling, for giving me the nudge to start using my own words and voice. In such a scary and vunerable process, you made me feel safe.

To Jeannette Bajalia, for lighting a fire in me to focus on and empower women in my world.

To David Bach, for recognizing decades ago that consulting and educating women was a worthwhile pursuit, especially when industry leaders told you it wasn't.

Finally, to my wonderful husband, Randy, for supporting me with your love while allowing me to grow and flourish. Thanks for faithfully serving and caring for our female clients, setting the greatest example, and keeping me laughing! I would not be here if it weren't for you and your commitment to me, us, our three boys, and our clients. My deepest desire is to make you proud.